PRAISE FOR *UNAFRAID*

"I want every American to read Adam Hamilton's *Unafraid*. There is no saccharine advice in this book, only honest assessments about the danger of nurturing fears and the power of facing them down."

—DIANA BUTLER BASS, author of *Grateful: The Transformative Power of Giving Thanks*

"A thoughtful, literate, faith-filled guide to reclaiming our minds and our lives."

—JOHN ORTBERG, senior pastor of Menlo Church, Menlo Park, CA, and author of *I'd Like You More If You Were More Like Me*

"Fear can cause us to become discouraged, disheartened, and even despairing. . . . In his bold new book, Adam Hamilton shows us a way out."

—JAMES MARTIN, SJ, author of *Jesus: A Pilgrimage*

"Informed by psychology and neuroscience, Hamilton applies practical wisdom gleaned from the Bible and from his years as a pastor. I could almost feel my blood pressure go down as I read."

—PHILIP YANCEY, author of *What's So Amazing About Grace?*

"An indispensable volume for people of faith who want to rise above dysfunction and uncertainty."

—MIKE MCCURRY, director of the Center for Public Theology, Wesley Seminary, and former White House press secretary

"A road map for facing our fears with faith. I highly recommend this book."

—RICHARD ROHR, author of *Falling Upward* and founder and director of the Center for Action and Contemplation, Albuquerque, NM

"Whatever challenge you're facing today, you will find Hamilton's words are comforting, practical, proven, and inspiring."

> —JOHN C. DANFORTH, former U.S. ambassador to the UN and former three-term U.S. senator from Missouri

"Read *Unafraid* once to appreciate its tremendous value. Read it again, as I did, to allow this consummate pastor to show you how to live with courage and hope."

> —MARIANN EDGAR BUDDE, bishop of the Episcopal Diocese of Washington

"A wise and compelling book."

> —MIROSLAV VOLF, founder and director of Yale Center for Faith and Culture, Yale Divinity School, and author of *Flourishing: Why We Need Religion in a Globalized World*

"Goes beyond mere analysis to offer spiritual practices that can bring real peace to struggling people. I enthusiastically recommend this book."

> —ED ROBB, senior pastor of the Woodlands United Methodist Church, Woodlands, TX

"Adam Hamilton has done it again, serving as a postmodern spiritual guide for a nation in desperate need of renewal. The mix of science, philosophy, practical biblical wisdom, storytelling, and personal testimony make this book a joy read."

> —OTIS MOSS III, senior servant/pastor of Trinity United Church of Christ, Chicago, IL

"I've known Adam for decades. I've watched him lead when he was fearful. In *Unafraid*, he writes, 'As you press through your fear, you live. . . .' He's right. Read *Unafraid*. Let Adam encourage you to face your fears and live."

> —MARK BEESON, founding pastor of Granger Community Church, Granger, IN

UNAFRAID

LIVING WITH COURAGE AND HOPE
IN UNCERTAIN TIMES

ADAM HAMILTON

CONVERGENT
NEW YORK

All rights reserved.
Published in the United States by Convergent Books, an imprint of the
Crown Publishing Group, a division of Penguin Random House LLC,
New York.
crownpublishing.com

CONVERGENT BOOKS is a registered trademark and its C colophon is
a trademark of Penguin Random House LLC.

Excerpt from *Hymn of Promise* by Natalie Sleeth copyright © 1986 Hope
Publishing Company, Carol Stream, IL 60188, www.hopepublishing.com.
All rights reserved. Used by permission.

Library of Congress Cataloging-in-Publication Data is available upon
request.

ISBN 978-1-5247-6033-5
Ebook ISBN 978-1-5247-6034-2

Printed in the United States of America

Book design by Lauren Dong
Jacket design by Jessie Sayward Bright
Page 11 illustration copyright © Florilegius/Mary Evans

10 9 8

To LaVon,
whose courage in the face of fear
inspired me to write this book

Contents

Part One: UNDERSTANDING AND COUNTERING
              FEAR

Chapter 1:   Afraid *3*

Chapter 2:   The Anatomy of Fear *10*

Chapter 3:   Paralyzed by Fear a Mile from the
              Promised Land *19*

Chapter 4:   Facing Your Fears *29*

Part Two: CRIME, RACE, TERRORISM, AND POLITICS

Chapter 5:   We Need a Security System *43*

Chapter 6:   Troost Avenue *55*

Chapter 7:   Weaponizing Fear *63*

Chapter 8:   The Sky Is Falling! *74*

Part Three: FAILURE, DISAPPOINTING OTHERS,
              INSIGNIFICANCE, AND LONELINESS

Chapter 9:   "But What If I Fail?" *85*

Chapter 10:   Desperate to Please *92*

Chapter 11:   Meaningless *104*

Chapter 12:   Alone and Unloved *115*

Part Four: APOCALYPSE, CHANGE, MISSING OUT,
              AND FINANCES

Chapter 13:   A Dystopian Future   *133*

Chapter 14:   We Never Did It That Way Before   *143*

Chapter 15:   FOMO   *150*

Chapter 16:   I Could Buy Me a Boat   *159*

Part Five: AGING, ILLNESS, DYING, AND FEAR OF
              THE LORD

Interlude: Siddhartha's Story   173

Chapter 17:   "I Don't Want to Grow Old!"   *176*

Chapter 18:   Anxiety, Worry, and Physical Illness   *188*

Chapter 19:   "I'm Not Ready to Die"   *208*

Chapter 20:   Living with Fear, Yet Unafraid   *223*

Acknowledgments   237

Appendix: 31 Days of Scripture Readings on Fear   239

Part One

UNDERSTANDING AND COUNTERING FEAR

1

Afraid

There are two basic motivating forces: fear and love . . .
all hopes for a better world rest in the fearlessness and
open-hearted vision of people who embrace life.

—JOHN LENNON

IN 1947, W. H. AUDEN PUBLISHED HIS PULITZER PRIZE—
winning book, *The Age of Anxiety*. If the postwar 1940s
and 1950s was the age of anxiety, ours might be appropriately
deemed the age of *high* anxiety.

We can hardly overstate the extent to which worry, anxiety,
and fear permeate our lives. We worry about the future, about
politics, and about our health. We fear violent crime, racial
divisions, and the future of the economy. Deep rifts in our nation leave us with an increasing sense of uncertainty. Fear in the
financial markets can wipe out billions of dollars of wealth in
a single day. Our fears, in the form of insecurity, often wreak
havoc on our lives and personal relationships. Google *fear* and
you'll find over six hundred million websites in 0.98 second.

My phone (and watch) vibrate multiple times each day with
"breaking news," most of it bad. Today alone I've been notified
of a subway bombing in Russia, continued conflict in Congress,
a constable shot in Texas, and three people killed in St. Louis
when a boiler exploded, and it's only noon. Stories from parts

of the world we'd be hard-pressed to find on a map show up in our newsfeeds in close to real time. Put enough of those stories together and it seems as if the world is going to the proverbial "hell in a handbasket." Molly Ball, writing in *The Atlantic,* notes, "Fear is in the air, and fear is surging. Americans are more afraid today than they have been in a long time."[*]

In preparation for a sermon series, I recently conducted a survey of the congregation at The United Methodist Church of the Resurrection, because I wanted to know how fear might be shaping the lives of my congregation. Of the 2,400 people who took the survey, nearly half reported living with a moderate level of fear, while 35 percent reported living with a *significant* amount of fear. *Eighty percent lived with moderate or significant levels of fear.* Those under age fifty experienced more fear than those over fifty. The greatest fear of those over fifty was the direction of our country. Fears of failure and of disappointing others topped the list for those younger than fifty.

Nearly two decades after 9/11, religious extremists continue to spread fear by committing occasional but highly publicized acts of violence. We're still recovering from the 2008 economic crisis that left millions unemployed and slashed the value of Americans' retirement savings by trillions. Many people live with the awareness of how quickly our economy and livelihoods can falter. We're polarized politically, with each side crying wolf on a daily basis. And then there are the universal worries people have felt in every age—concerns for our children, fear of failure, anxiety about death and dying and so much more.

---

[*] Molly Ball, "Donald Trump and the Politics of Fear," *The Atlantic,* September 2, 2016.

WHAT FEAR LOOKS LIKE FROM HERE

I've seen this climate of fear up close, as a long-time pastor of a large congregation planted squarely in mid-America. I've noticed that men are often hesitant to admit that they feel fearful because it seems to be a sign of weakness. Instead we talk about being "stressed." But if you poke around our stress a bit to look for what's driving us, you'll find worry and anxiety—sometimes outright panic.

Years ago, I went to my internist because I was experiencing tightness in my chest. I dismissed the chest pains at first, but my wife, LaVon, asked me to please go to the doctor. After a series of tests, he told me my heart was fine, but he asked about my stress level. It was at an all-time high. I was leading a capital campaign at the church raising funds to construct the church's sanctuary. I hadn't had a day off in ages, and I was working sixty-plus hours a week. I admitted to the doctor that there were times I felt that the success or failure of the entire effort rested on me.

My doctor said, "No wonder you're having chest pains! Listen, your heart is okay for now, but if you don't figure out how to deal with this stress, it might well eventually affect your heart."

Both men and women wrestle with insecurities, one of fear's many faces. Like most people, I've learned to put a good face on my insecurities and (mostly) keep them to myself. But I'm surprised by how often this fear gnaws at me. Each week I stand before my congregation to deliver a thirty-minute message intended to teach, encourage, and inspire them. I've delivered thousands of messages in weekend worship, as well as at funerals, college baccalaureate services and commencement ceremonies, even the National Prayer Service for President

Obama's second inauguration. Yet, starting every Tuesday and continuing until I've preached the last of five weekend services on Sunday, I feel a persistent, gnawing anxiety that stems from my fear of failure—failing God, failing my congregation, and embarrassing myself. (I believe the fear of humiliation is the reason why public speaking consistently ranks among people's top fears.)

My anxiety about failing in the pulpit occasionally shows up in my dreams, or nightmares, sometimes in humorous ways. From time to time I have a dream that the phone is ringing. Someone is calling from the church wondering why I'm still in bed when it's Sunday morning and service has begun. I frantically get ready, drive to the church, and run to the pulpit just in time to deliver the message. But there is no manuscript waiting for me—nothing to say. Just then I hear people laughing. I glance down and see that I've forgotten to get completely dressed. I'm standing in front of the congregation in my boxers!

The fear of preaching in my boxers rates pretty low among things that worry me, but it represents, in my subconscious, the fear of public humiliation.

THE EMOTION THAT PROFOUNDLY SHAPES US

The reality is everyone worries about something. We all have things we fear. And most of us will have seasons when anxieties and fear simply overwhelm us. Fear is a powerful emotion that shapes all of us in profound ways we often don't fully understand. Look behind depression's door and you'll often find fear. Addictions too. Peer beneath broken marriages and friendships, beneath prejudice and hate, and you'll find fear. And look behind the causes of most wars throughout human history and you'll find lurking behind all of the other reasons,

2

The Anatomy of Fear

There is no greater hell than to be a prisoner of fear.

—BEN JONSON

LET'S BEGIN BY ACKNOWLEDGING THAT OUR BODY'S CA-
pacity to experience fear, and our ability to respond to
perceived threats, when working properly, are absolutely amazing. This marvel of nature, which I receive as a gift from God,
is often referred to as the fight-or-flight response. You've no
doubt experienced it on many occasions. When I was eleven
years old, while riding my bike to school, an angry dog shot out
from someone's yard with every intention—I thought—to eat
my leg. For a moment, I had superhuman strength. I pedaled
faster than my Schwinn had ever gone before, and for a little
while, faster than that dog. Fortunately for me and my heart
rate, the dog gave up the chase.

Our five senses—sight, hearing, smell, taste, and touch—
alongside other less familiar senses we possess, send signals to
the brain's amygdala, two almond-shaped structures, one nestled deep on each side of the brain. These structures have been
described as the "center for emotions, emotional behavior, and
motivation" within the brain.* Before your conscious mind has

---

* Neuroscience Online, http://neuroscience.uth.tmc.edu/s4/chapter06.html.

fear, often manufactured by the leaders who led their people to
wage war.

Often we fear things that will never happen; yet real or
imagined, these fears have power. Sometimes our battles with
fear take a more serious turn, becoming a debilitating struggle
with panic attacks or anxiety disorders. There are other times
when fear is well placed, and people have good reason to be
afraid: they are facing life-threatening illnesses, the impending
death of a loved one, potentially devastating legal conflicts, or
significant economic distress.

Fear isn't simply an American phenomenon: it is universal.
My ministry has taken me around the world. I've found that
people living in villages in Zimbabwe and Malawi, with none
of our modern technology or first-world problems, struggle
with fear. People in Haiti and Honduras have described for me
their struggle with fear. And no religion or philosophy relieves
us entirely of fear: Buddhists, Muslims, Jews, atheists, and agnostics, along with Christians, struggle with fear.

I've seen firsthand in the lives of people I love how fear can
imprison us, paralyze us, and keep us from experiencing a ful-
filling and joyful life. It was during a conversation with a friend
that I first realized how much I needed to study and write about
fear—both for myself and for others. I'll tell you my friend's
story later, but as he described what it was like to feel completely overwhelmed by the fear of failure, stories of others who
had conveyed similar struggles flooded my mind and reminded
me of the very real scope of the problem. Before long, I was
reading the work of experts in the field of fear. I spent time
with people in my own congregation who have suffered terribly
from anxiety, worry, and other kinds of fear. In addition to the
survey I conducted with my congregation, I analyzed the latest
national polls to see what people across the country rank as

their top fears. I studied the many passages of scripture related to fear, and the way in which faith and spiritual disciplines have played a key role in helping people I know to find peace in the face of their fears. The book you're holding is the result.

No, I don't have the silver bullet that will keep you from ever feeling fear again (no one else does, either). For reasons we'll see in the next chapter, you can never fully eliminate fear from your life (and that's actually a good thing). The battle with fear is not a one-and-done kind of battle; rather, it is a regular part of our lives. But while fear is a persistent companion, we don't have to be controlled by it. We can learn to address our fears, control them, learn from them, even use them, and we can press through them.

THE PRACTICAL PROMISE OF UNAFRAID

In the pages ahead we'll look at both what the experts can teach us about overcoming fear and how people from time immemorial have addressed their fears. Modern psychology has drawn from this ancient wisdom and often improved upon it with new insights from science coupled with clinical experience on how to cope with fear. I'll share with you some of the most helpful approaches for dealing with worry, fear, and anxiety.

I've spent the last thirty years shepherding my congregation and in the process becoming deeply involved with their struggles with fear of failure, irrelevance, illness, growing old, and death, to name a few that we'll consider in this book. I've had the privilege of walking with them through economic downturns, two wars, terrorist attacks, and more personal tragedies than I can count. Together we've found consistent insight and comfort from the Christian faith we share and a variety of spiritual practices. I'll share those with you too.

One of the most repeated instructions in the Bible is "Don't be afraid." These words, in one form or another, appear over 140 times in scripture. They remind us that ordinary women and men from the age of Israel's patriarchs to first-century Christians struggled with fear. But they also show us that faith can be pivotal to overcoming fear and finding peace in uncertain times. In this book, we'll consider scripture passages about fear and the spiritual practices that can bring real peace. If you're not a particularly religious person, that's okay—you'll still find plenty of helpful material here. But if you are open to insights from Jewish and Christian scriptures and practices, I think you'll see how the spiritual dimension of life holds a particularly potent key to overcoming fear.

Most of us have known times when fear, worry, or anxiety has robbed us of the life we wanted. At times it has led us to make bad decisions. Sometimes it has kept us from taking risks or doing things that would have brought great meaning, fulfillment, and joy to our lives. You can never completely eradicate fear—you need it. But fear doesn't have to control you. As we'll consider later in the book, courage is not the absence of fear; instead, it is doing what you feel you should do, or what you long to do, despite the fear. As you press through your fear, you live a life of courage and hope.

fully made sense of what you have heard, felt, seen, smelled, or tasted, your amygdala has already made an initial determination as to whether what you've sensed is a threat. And if it *is* perceived as a threat, the amygdala activates your body's early warning system, releasing chemicals like epinephrine (adrenaline) and cortisol, the hormone commonly associated with stress.

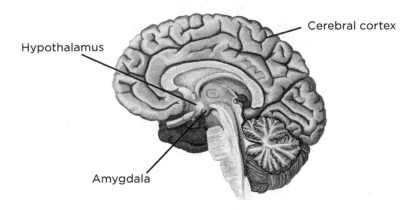

Hypothalamus

Cerebral cortex

Amygdala

These signals, along with other hormones released as a result of activity in your amygdala, create a cascade of physiological effects meant to save your life if you are in danger. Your heart begins to race, your breathing becomes more rapid and more shallow, your mouth gets dry, your muscles tense up—all aimed at helping you fight or flee. You will likely shake and perspire, your pupils will dilate, and you may even wet yourself—this is all part of the reaction to the hormones flowing through your system to prepare your body for action. In the moment you may lose peripheral vision and some hearing; these hormones also produce feelings of anxiety, dread, or aggression. If you struggle with panic attacks and anxiety, you will recognize a number of these symptoms.

Our responses to a perceived danger happen almost

instantaneously—before the rational mind can process the experience. It explains why you can jump out of the way of an oncoming car before you've even fully comprehended the danger with your conscious mind.

MAYBELLE CHARGES; THE OPOSSUM FREEZES

This reactive capacity is found not just in humans but in all animals to varying degrees. It is why the opossum that lives under my front step freezes when my little dog, Maybelle, comes charging outside barking at its scent (and why, when freezing doesn't stop my dog from barking, the opossum bares its teeth and hisses). It is also why my dog runs barking and charging at the opossum (as well as at the raccoons that live out back). Maybelle—all seven pounds of her—is rising to a perceived threat. Maybelle charges. The opossum freezes.

Here's where things get interesting: The brain, including the amygdala, has the ability to learn to associate various sensations—sounds, smells, tastes, sights, touches, even people and places or other experiences—with past events, both good and bad. This ability to connect one sensory experience or stimulus with something else—something desirable or something dangerous or frightening—is called classical conditioning.

Ivan Pavlov, the brilliant Russian scientist whose name you no doubt recognize, won the Nobel Prize in 1904 for his work with dog saliva. Pavlov knew why dogs salivated when presented with food—it is a biological response, necessary for the dog's digestion. But in the course of conducting his experiment, Pavlov noticed that his canine subjects began to salivate when the people who fed them walked into the room, even if they brought no food.

Pavlov began ringing a bell when food was presented. After doing this for some time, he then rang the bell without presenting food and found the dogs salivated anyway. The dogs had come to associate an unrelated sensation—the sound of the bell—with the presentation of food. The idea is universally understood today, but in 1904, it was a pretty big insight.

The importance of this insight was about more than how dogs salivate. Pavlov's discovery showed how our brains can come to associate a neutral stimulus with something else that's completely unrelated. This goes for all five senses—sounds, smells, sights, tastes, touches—and all kinds of other experiences.

APPLE MUNCHIES OVER THE GRAND CANYON

On a family vacation one summer, we took a plane ride over the Grand Canyon. An hour earlier I had bought a bag of dried apple slices coated in cinnamon and sugar—they were homemade snacks at the campground we were staying at, given the sophisticated label "Apple Munchies." We took off and soon came to the edge of the Grand Canyon, where we encountered strong updrafts that shook and swayed our little aircraft. I instantly wished I had not been snacking on those apples. Not long after this, our pilot, wanting to make sure we saw all the beauty of the canyon, began banking the plane, first one way and then the other, so we could see the entire beauty of this amazing place. Before long I reached for one of those little motion sickness bags in the seatback pocket, and you can guess what came next. It took several hours after deplaning before my stomach calmed down. To this day I no longer eat "Apple Munchies." The dried apples had nothing to do with my getting sick on the plane—I could have eaten any number of things with the same result. But I still get queasy when I think about eating dried apple snacks.

In the same way, when you have had a traumatic experience in the past, and that experience was associated with a smell, a sight, a sound, a taste, a feeling, a person, or a place, your brain might come to associate that stimulus with the unpleasant, frightening, or painful situation. You respond to the same stimulus later with fear, but for reasons you may not be able to explain, or even understand, regardless of whether there is any real danger.

Why? Because this particular stimulus is still associated, in your subconscious memory, with a past threat. Though there is no real danger, the threat switchboard that is your amygdala is still lighting up.

ETHAN'S STORY

Ethan, a young man in his twenties, became anxious when he was near water—lakes, oceans, even swimming pools. He did a good job of hiding it. He tried to avoid situations where he would have to be on or near the water. One day, while he was on vacation in California with friends, his buddies suggested they take a sunset cruise. As the time drew closer, Ethan thought he might be having a heart attack—he had chest pains, his heart was pounding, he was short of breath, and he was overwhelmed with a feeling of dread. He ended up in the emergency room with his friends. The doctors ran a battery of tests, but they found nothing. After this experience, he spoke to his parents about his anxiety around water. They told him that when he was three years old, he fell into a neighbor's swimming pool and nearly drowned. Ethan had no recollection of the incident, but the terror of it had lain dormant in his subconscious until that night, decades later, as he prepared to take a sunset cruise.

In a book that proposes to address the problem of fear, I want us first to see its promise. With almost no conscious help from us, fear tries to keep us safe. In his bestselling book *The Gift of Fear,* Gavin de Becker called fear "a brilliant internal guardian." Before we try to address the challenges with this system, we all ought to show some gratitude.

The stimulus that leads the amygdala to kick off the series of reactions that put our body on high alert, resulting in our experience of fear or anxiety, is often referred to as a trigger. As we've seen, these triggers are set off by data from our five senses that the amygdala perceives as a potential threat. We're all data collectors, in this sense, for our entire lives. Which is a good thing too, because the data, along with the fears associated with it, keeps us out of harm's way.

THE GIFT OF HEALTHY FEARS

When I was seven, I did something that was really stupid, but for some reason it didn't seem stupid to my seven-year-old brain. After watching my parents plug things into wall outlets, I decided to see what exactly happened when you insert a random metal object into an outlet. I'd like to think I was being scientifically curious. How did this thing really work? As I recall, I had a small hand trowel with a sharp point on the end given to me by my grandmother (she loved gardening and hoped I would pick up the hobby). One day I sat in my room and conducted the experiment. I put the pointed end of the trowel into the outlet in my bedroom. Zap! I hurtled backward. Sparks shot from the outlet, and smoke, and the lights went out in part of the house. Fortunately for me, the trowel had a rubber handle. But the experience terrified me.

Soon I heard my dad heading down the hall asking, "What the hell just happened?" I quickly hid the trowel in my toy box. When he came in he could smell the smoke and see the charred outlet. He asked again, "What happened?" My seven-year-old self said, "I don't know" (which, to some degree, was true!). He then asked, "What did you put in the outlet?" to which I replied, "Nothing" (which, of course, was not true). He opened my toy box, found the trowel blackened on the end, and proceeded to "put the fear of God" in me. I didn't understand then what I know today—he was scared that I could have seriously hurt myself, and he needed me to feel that fear so that I would never again put anything into an outlet that shouldn't be in one. And it worked!

Consider these healthy fears: Fear of falling to our death keeps us from getting too close to the edge of a cliff. A fear of heart disease should motivate us to eat better and exercise. Fear of fast-moving objects and the possibility of our bodily harm causes us to duck when something is thrown at us. And a fear of living in poverty when we're old leads us to sacrifice and save for retirement when we're young. I'm profoundly grateful for fear and its power to motivate me to act, and its gift of the ability to quickly react.

Real fear, as the title of de Becker's book suggests, is a gift that has the power to save our lives. Unfortunately, much of our fear is manufactured; our worries are about things that are likely never going to happen or things completely outside of our control. This fear, anxiety, or worry is not a gift; it brings harm instead.

De Becker tries to help his readers pay attention to, and gain clarity about, real dangers, then train their instincts and fight-or-flight mechanism to work properly. In the case of domestic violence, rape, and assault cases, he notes that often there are warning signs and intuitions that are dismissed. De Becker's career has included training many, particularly high-profile, women on how to recognize the warning signals, to pay attention to their intuition in order to avoid dangerous situations or to escape them when they come. "Intuition," de Becker notes, "is always right in at least two important ways; it is always in response to something [and] it always has your best interest at heart."

Obviously, even at the level of intuition, fear is intended to help us sense and avoid danger. But it's also true that we often misread signals, worry about threats that are not real, and find ourselves overwhelmed by false fears, paralyzing anxiety, or unhealthy fretting concerning things that (a) we don't need to be afraid of, (b) will never happen, or (c) worrying and fear can do nothing to save us from.

So we recognize the good gift of fear, and the importance of paying attention to our intuition and being able to detect and respond to real danger. But from here on out we're going to focus on false fears and unhealthy worry, because, as Ethan's story illustrates, our learned responses can actually keep us from living well. And as all those who struggle with seemingly random attacks of anxiety and panic can attest, they can bring more harm than good. But we can find good news, even here. We can change our fear-based conditioning. We can—as Pavlov's dogs also showed—*un*learn.

You see, once a dog made the connection between the ringing of the bell and food, Pavlov found that if he consistently rang the bell and presented *no* food to the dog, over time the dog would eventually stop salivating on cue. Psychologists call this fading of the link between the bell and salivating "extinction." Extinction is usually a negative term associated with the end of various animal or plant species on earth. But when applied to eliminating worry, fear, or anxiety based on old or inaccurate data in our lives, extinction holds out the promise that we can move on. We can *un*learn fear, and in unlearning fear we can find freedom.

3

Paralyzed by Fear a Mile from the Promised Land

"The land we explored consumes those living in it.
All the people we saw in the land were giants. . . .
We seemed like grasshoppers in our eyes, and we looked
that way to them as well."

—NUMBERS 13:32–33

THE BIBLE IS FILLED WITH STORIES OF PEOPLE WHOSE fears got the best of them. One that has always fascinated me is recorded in Numbers 13–14.

In dramatic fashion, through plagues and the parting of the sea, God liberated the Israelites from hundreds of years of slavery in Egypt. Pharaoh's army, arguably the most powerful of the time, with the most advanced weaponry, had just been decimated by God's miraculous intervention. Once liberated, Moses then cast a vision of a Promised Land for these former slaves, a land "flowing with milk and honey" that God had vowed he would give to his people. The land of Canaan, the Promised Land, lay north of the Sinai, where the freed slaves now camped. Two years after leaving Egypt, the Israelites had made their way to Kadesh Barnea, just a mile south of Canaan. They were ready to take possession of God's promise.

There's a lesson for us in what came next. Before entering the land, the Israelites sent twelve spies, who for forty days explored the area and contemplated how they would expel the nations that currently inhabited this land promised by God to their ancestor Abraham hundreds of years before. Upon returning, two of the spies said, in effect, "It's all there, just like God promised. And it's awesome! God is with us—let's go get it!" But then the other ten spies spoke up. "We can't go and take the land," they said. "The city walls are strong, the people are even stronger. They look like the giants of old, and we look like insects, mere grasshoppers compared to them!"

And with that, the same people who had witnessed God's deliverance from the mighty Egyptians began to weep and suggest it was time to give up. Some even argued that they should go back to Egypt and return to a life of slavery!

THE PUSH AND PULL OF HOPE AND DREAD

Can you relate to the powerful push and pull of hope and dread in God's people? Have you ever found yourself terrified of some kind of "giants" that seemed insurmountable—circumstances in the face of which you felt like giving up before you even got started? Can you see yourself in their story?

In the end, the Israelites did not go back to slavery in Egypt. But they did remain camped in the desert in and around Kadesh Barnea—for the next *thirty-eight years*! It wasn't until the next generation arose that the children of Israel finally entered the Promised Land. Can you imagine, for thirty-eight years they remained paralyzed by fear just a mile from the Promised Land.

I love the story because it paints a picture of how fear works in us. We start out with a vision of a Promised Land—our preferred picture of the future, something we long to do, a dream or a calling to pursue—but then we begin to think about the risks and dangers involved. Soon all we can see are the obstacles, risks, and dangers. We freeze in our tracks. Terror and despair take over. We wish we could turn back. We tell ourselves, "I could never do that. I don't have what it takes. What if I fail? Others are far more gifted than I am. It's just too hard."

But what if—as the story of the Israelites later, long-delayed conquest of Canaan revealed—the obstacles, risks, and dangers that daunt us appear *much more formidable than they really are*?

I think about the warning etched into the side mirrors of our cars in America: objects in the mirror are closer than they appear. This is a helpful warning—the convex shape of the mirror does make things appear smaller and thus seemingly farther away than they really are. That can lead us to miscalculate lane changes if we don't take this into account. But when it comes to our assessment of risk, dangers, and obstacles, often the opposite is true: obstacles, dangers, and threats appear *larger* and *closer* than they really are. The obstacles seem like giants, and we mere grasshoppers.

So many of us live our entire lives paralyzed by fear, just a mile from the Promised Land. I find that this is true for us as individuals, it is true in organizations, and it is true at times for nations. Can you recall some critical time in your past when you were stuck for long stretches of your life in the mire of fear? You might even be there right now.

It was the night before my wedding, and I was becoming increasingly anxious. My parents had divorced when I was a kid. My mom and stepdad had divorced. LaVon and I were way too young to be getting married. We had $300 to our name after we prepaid the first month's rent. We owned two clunker cars and had one part-time job between the two of us. I'd been accepted to college in Tulsa, but didn't yet know what kind of financial aid or scholarships I might receive. Somehow, being young and married and broke had seemed okay to me until that night after the wedding rehearsal. Now it seemed impossibly stupid, no matter how much I loved LaVon.

That was thirty-five years ago, and, as I look back, our headlong naïveté still seems incredibly stupid! But somehow things worked out. The giants were not really giants, we worked hard, scholarships came in, we got jobs, we lived frugally, and we survived. Today, we look back on the challenges as an adventure that brought us closer together. And while LaVon and I took more than our share of risks when we married, every marriage comes with risks, obstacles, and potential dangers.

STARING DOWN YOUR GIANTS

Look at any successful person, however you define success, and you'll find someone who knew fear. They have faced their share of giants. They've felt like turning back and been paralyzed by fear. What differentiated them from others is that they realized—or at least hoped—the giants were not really giants. They took a realistic view of the risks, dangers, and obstacles and believed there was at least a reasonable chance they could overcome them.

Mark Zuckerberg, Facebook's founder and CEO, noted the best bit of advice he'd ever received was from PayPal cofounder Peter Thiel: "The biggest risk you can take is not taking any risk."[*]

Your amygdala is risk-averse. Its job is to identify risks, dangers, and obstacles and to protect you from them. This can be a wonderful blessing and can save your life, but it can also

---

[*] Kathleen Elkins, "Mark Zuckerberg Shares the Best Piece of Advice Peter Thiel Ever Gave Him," CNBC.com, August 25, 2016.

keep you from living. Your amygdala's job is to consider the worst—to see the ordinary Canaanites as undefeatable giants.

But at some point you've got to face the giants, stare them down, see if they really are as big and bad as your amygdala—or others around you—have said. If they are, then you had better listen, and you might want to fight, flee, or freeze. But usually you'll find the risks, dangers, and obstacles appear larger and more formidable than they really are.

In 1987, the singer George Michael was making a play for a solo career after a successful five-year run in the teen heart-throb band Wham! His first solo album, which went on to sell over twenty million copies, was called *Faith,* from the hit song by the same name.

The song wasn't about religious faith. Michael sang of having been hurt in a recent relationship and his uncertainty about entering into a new one just to be hurt all over again. Should he settle for a relationship he didn't really want to be in, simply because he was afraid no one else would come along? No, in the end he had to have faith that he would find real love again: You gotta have faith.

Faith in this sense is trust, confidence, hope, or belief that, regardless of your current circumstances or your recent experiences, things will get better, that things will turn out okay. George Michael is right: when you are walking through troubled times, even if you are not a religious person, you gotta have faith.

What is the alternative to faith that things will work out, that they'll get better, that there will be another chance? I suppose it would be pessimism, hopelessness, or despair. For those Israelites camped in the desert, the alternative to faith was paralysis.

When fear begins to control us, it's often because we have

"catastrophized" our current situation. In other words, we are seeing things as worse than they really are, and we're assuming they will never get better. (Which, if you think about it, is a kind of faith in reverse: of all the possible outcomes and without knowing all the facts, you are choosing to hold on to the unwanted ones and to believe the worst instead of the best.)

JEFF MAKES A PLAN

Jeff, a corporate executive in my congregation, had just lost his job; a corporate merger had made his role redundant and therefore expendable. He'd received a modest severance package and was now hunting for employment. After just a few weeks, he found fear began to creep into his thoughts: "They didn't keep me because they figured out that I'm really not competent. I'm not getting callbacks because there are many more qualified people than me. I'm never again going to have a job that pays what my last job paid. I'm forty-one and it's all downhill from here. We'll need to sell the house. My kids won't be able to go to college. We'll never be able to retire. . . ." By the time he'd cycled through these thoughts, his heart was pounding and he felt paralyzed by fear.

The giants were getting bigger and bigger, and Jeff was looking more and more like a grasshopper every day. He was in need of a little faith—faith in himself, faith in his ability to bring something of value to a company, faith that things weren't really as bad as they seemed.

But to find that faith, he had to stare down the giants and take on each of his fears. He found it most helpful to do this in writing. He began by writing down his fears, the thoughts that he was ruminating on. He went back over the annual reviews he'd had since he started with his previous company—

they were generally quite good. He read the positive comments his bosses had made about him. Maybe he wasn't let go because he was incompetent.

He made a list of his skills and passions, things that might be valuable outside of his previous career track. He began brainstorming places where he might work, and how his family could tighten their belts to allow him to take a lower-paying job that had promise in the event that one was offered to him. He set a realistic time frame for finding a new job—months, not weeks. And he wrote down a plan of attack for finding a new job—what he would do each day from nine to five in his search. All of these things gave a boost to his morale and helped him ward off the fears.

Jeff's experience gives us a helpful insight. It is not enough to simply have faith that things will work out. You've also got to act. I'm reminded of the words of Saint James in the New Testament: "What good is it if you have faith but don't have works?" (James 2:14) and "Faith, without works, is dead" (James 2:17). He was writing about something completely different—a first-century debate concerning salvation: does salvation come only by faith, or do works play a role? But if we think of salvation as deliverance (which is another way of translating the Greek word for salvation), our deliverance from fear comes by having faith *and* by acting on it. I've found that as long as people are paralyzed and have no plan, the problems seem bigger and the anxiety only grows.

If you find yourself in a situation something like Jeff's, he might pass on a few tips: Choose to believe that things can work out. Look squarely at those big, ugly giants, one at a time; then put down in writing a detailed plan for defeating them. "Do that," Jeff would tell you, "and you're already most of the way home."

Jeff ended up making a complete career change after three months of searching. It did mean a reduction in pay at first. His family tightened their belts, sold a car to get out from a payment, developed a budget (which they had always meant to do but had never done), and simplified their lives a bit. When we spoke again several months later, Jeff was not the same guy. He told me he loved his new job. He hadn't realized how unhappy he had been doing what he was doing before. Of all the things he had feared, none had come to pass.

FALSE EVENTS APPEARING REAL

That's how it is with most of the things we fear. We spend a lot of time and emotional energy worrying about and fearing things that will never happen. You're likely familiar with the acronym for these specific kinds of fears:

False
Events
Appearing
Real

In the pages ahead, we'll look at how both contemporary science and a better grasp of facts can help defeat fears of every kind. And we'll go beyond the lyrics of a George Michael song to show how a deeply rooted faith in God can literally change our lives. Faith of this sort empowers millions to live with courage in the face of real fear and extreme difficulties—and I'm confident it can help you too.

As a Christian pastor, I want you to understand what I *don't* mean by that much-abused word *faith*.

I'm not, for example, talking about a saccharine faith that assures us that if we pray hard enough nothing bad will ever happen to us. As a pastor, I've walked with enough people through hell to know that this is not how life works. I am not proposing the theologically inaccurate view that everything that happens is the will of God. And I won't insult you by suggesting that if only you have enough faith, you'll never have fears. But I will suggest that a well-considered faith in God and the timeless insights of scripture can have a profound impact on your ability to experience peace, hope, and joy despite your fears.

A WELL-CONSIDERED FAITH

My life experience, the experience of others I've known, and the bold assertions of the Christian faith persuade me that God never abandons us in our darkest hours. Instead, God has a mysterious way of working through even the tragedies of life to accomplish his purposes.

That's why I can propose another acronym that captures four important steps we'll consider in the pages ahead:*

Face your fears with faith.
Examine your assumptions in light of the facts.
Attack your anxieties with action.
Release your cares to God.

Of course, that practiced, articulate, and noisy doubter who chatters incessantly in your head is already at work. *Four dumb steps? An acronym, for crying out loud? Clearly, this guy doesn't have a clue what I'm up against!*

---

* Dozens of acronyms suggesting how we can address and overcome FEAR have been proposed. My variation is inspired by many others.

And I don't. But I do know that what your inner doomsayer fears most is that you'll take one small step of faith: You reach for pen and paper. You make the call. You decide you'll take a risk to get your life back. You look your giant in the eye. And with that step, you're already in motion. Ralph Waldo Emerson wrote, "Do the thing we fear, and the death of fear is certain." That's what the next chapter is about.

4

Facing Your Fears

You gain strength, courage, and confidence by every experience in which you really stop to look fear in the face. You are able to say to yourself, "I lived through this horror. I can take the next thing that comes along."

—ELEANOR ROOSEVELT

BEHAVIORAL SCIENTISTS HAVE IDENTIFIED AND NAMED a tactic that human beings have used to combat fear likely for as long as we've walked this earth. They call it exposure therapy. But most of us would call it "confronting" or "facing" our fears.

When we feel anxious about something, we often avoid it. We try not to think about that conversation we've been meaning to have with our boss or the rent check due next month, but somewhere beneath the surface, the worry and anxiety continue to build. Exposure therapy breaks this cycle by calling on you to clearly identify the source of your fear or anxiety and then slowly face your fears by exposing yourself to them—at first with small steps, then gradually increasing the experience of exposure.

While writing this chapter, I heard a story on National Public Radio's *This American Life* about a ten-year-old girl named Tess who was terrified of roller coasters. Her father, a radio journalist named Bob Carlson, helped her conquer this fear by taking her to a Six Flags amusement park, where he told her they'd ride a child's roller coaster. At first, the thought of riding the coaster terrified Tess, but her father assured her it was safe. It was built for little children; surely she would survive this.

Tess did survive the coaster, and to her surprise, it wasn't even as scary as she imagined. In fact, it was kind of fun. So they moved on to a bigger coaster and then a bigger one, finally ending up at a nine-story-tall monster with two upside-down loops. Bob recorded the experience of Tess shouting, screaming, and—at the end of the ride—her exhilaration as she gushed, "I just rode a looping roller coaster for the first time in my life. And it wasn't even that bad. I am a different person than I was a minute ago!"

DANIELLE TAKES A FLYING LEAP

My daughter Danielle did something similar while enrolled at Kansas State University. Unbeknownst to her mother and me, she joined the skydiving club. She only told us about it after the fact, knowing that her new hobby would produce intense anxiety in her parents. I asked her why in the world she would do something like that and she said, "Dad, I joined the skydiving club as a way of confronting all of life's fears head-on, in one act. I knew that in my family I was genetically predisposed to anxiety, and I wanted to take preventative measures to keep fear from being a governing force in my life."

She made seven solo jumps out of a little Cessna. She described them to me:

As a trainee, the jump began by the instructor throwing open the door of the plane next to which you were sitting.

Being on the edge of the plane looking out at the ground below was terrifying and exhilarating. Once you worked up the courage, you would grab on to a bar that connected the wing of the plane to the body and pull yourself out so that you were flying along parallel to the plane for a few seconds while you got your body into a spread-eagle position. Then, you let go. It is a totally unique vantage point from which to view the world—calm and removed from all worry and chaos, a place where you can be a simple observer. Once your feet touch the ground the rush returns and you feel like you could do anything; after all, you have looked death in the face and said "not today."

Most of the things we're afraid of are not nearly as frightening as they seem, but the only way we'll learn this is to face our fears with faith—faith that we'll survive the roller coaster, faith that our parachute will open and allow us to fall slowly to the earth.

I'll admit that confronting your fears is not always the right way of addressing them. I wouldn't want to address my fear of rattlesnakes with exposure therapy! But for many of our fears, facing them liberates us, which is what Ralph Waldo Emerson meant when he said, "Do the thing we fear, and death of fear is certain."

Many people attack their anxieties and fears by taking medication, which can be really helpful, especially for those who struggle with anxiety disorders, panic attacks, obsessive-compulsive disorder, or even post-traumatic stress. And, as we've begun to see, therapists can offer important insights into how we can address our fears and find relief. But thousands of years before Freud, Jung, and Skinner offered their observations about the human mind, and before the world was introduced to Xanax, Zoloft, and Klonopin—medicines intended to treat anxiety and fear—the primary place human beings turned to find relief from fear was their faith in God and the spiritual practices that helped them to sense God's presence.

"FOR I AM WITH YOU"

Fear, and finding peace in the face of it, is one of the major themes of the Bible. The words *fear* or *afraid* appear over four hundred times in scripture. The people of biblical times had a lot to be afraid of: wild animals, illness, enemies, wars, bandits, the occasional earthquake, floods, droughts, famine, death at childbirth, death by disease, and a world that felt infinitely more dangerous and less predictable than our world today precisely because it was not understood.

Yet, as we noted in chapter 1, God's instruction "Do not be afraid" appears more than a hundred times in the Bible. These words were most often spoken in frightening or unnerving situations—times of national disaster, or when Israel's enemies were attacking, or when the people were asked by God to step out on faith and do the very thing they feared most. They were spoken in the midst of storms, when facing death, and when a situation seemed hopeless. But the phrase that often follows these words is just as important. God says to his people, "Do not be afraid, *for I am with you.*"

Let's return to the story of the Israelites camped a mile from the Promised Land. Twelve spies had been sent to explore the land and to bring back a report. Ten of them were terrified and frightened the people by reporting on the fortification of the cities and the size of the Canaanites. But two of them, Caleb and Joshua, offered a different perspective. Listen to what they said after hearing the report of the other spies:

The land we crossed through to explore is an exception-
ally good land. If the LORD *is pleased with us, he'll bring*
us into this land and give it to us. It's a land that's full
of milk and honey. Only don't rebel against the LORD
and don't be afraid of the people of the land. They are
our prey. Their defense has deserted them, but the LORD
is with us. So don't be afraid of them. (emphasis added)
(Numbers 14:7–9)

Did you catch that last line? "The LORD is with us. So don't
be afraid of them." For the Israelites who had just seen God
deliver them from the Egyptians, and who had been assured
that God would be with them in their fight with the Canaanites, their faith—their confidence and trust in God—should
have fundamentally changed their perspective on the giants in
the land of Canaan. If they had trusted God, they would have
looked at the Canaanites and understood that, when compared
to the God who parted the Red Sea, the Canaanites were the
ones who looked like grasshoppers!

When I was growing up, I lived in a neighborhood where
most of the kids were two or three years older than I was. At
times some of the older boys picked on me. One time, when I
was eight or nine, a couple of them grabbed me and tied me to
a chain-link fence behind a neighbor's house. They thought this
was great fun. I sat there for what seemed like hours until someone heard me calling and set me free. One of these neighborhood kids had an older brother named Bruce. For some reason
Bruce felt sorry for me, and he began sticking up for me. At one
point Bruce told these boys that if they were going to pick on
me, they'd have to deal with him. This fundamentally changed
my life—I was no longer afraid. I was in the third grade. The
older kids were fifth graders, but Bruce was in the seventh or

eighth grade. The balance of power had shifted in my favor, but not because I'd learned karate or been lifting weights. It shifted because Bruce had stepped in as my protector. That's how Joshua and Caleb saw things as they urged the Israelites to move ahead in taking the Promised Land. They were acting in faith on God's promise to be with them. God's presence and power radically changed how they faced their fears.

The same promise from God shows up hundreds of years later in another time of great fear. In 586 BC, the Babylonian armies destroyed Jerusalem and subsequently forced many of the Israelites to resettle in Babylon (modern-day Iraq). They were helpless against the power of the Babylonian Empire. But things were about to change. Within decades, Cyrus the Great of Persia (600–530 BC) and his armies would conquer the Babylonian Empire and pretty much every other empire in his path. Years before the battle for Babylon began, God told the Israelites,

> *Don't fear, because I am with you;*
> *don't be afraid, for I am your God.*
> *I will strengthen you,*
> *I will surely help you;*
> *I will hold you*
> *with my righteous strong hand.*
>
> (ISAIAH 41:10)

God *was* with them. After conquering the Babylonians, Cyrus issued an edict allowing the Jews to return to their homeland and providing support for the rebuilding of Jerusalem and the temple located there. It was astounding and something the Jews believed only God could have orchestrated. They had virtually no hope of ever returning home had it not been for Cyrus and the Persian army. The writer of Isaiah went so far as to call Cyrus God's messiah (45:1). And that offers us an insight into how God works. The biblical authors recognized that God didn't typically send angels to deliver his people. Nor did God's deliverance always come quickly. Instead God worked deliberately and through people, even unexpected people like Persian kings. *Don't let your fears get the better of you,* God wanted his people to know. *I am with you. I will help you.*

PRAYING THE SCRIPTURES

When I read scriptures, I trust that what God said to his people in the past, he may well say to us today. I may even use a text as a way of entering into a conversation with God:

> GOD: Don't fear, because I am with you; don't be afraid, for I am your God.

> ME: Thank you, Lord, for being with me always; help me to trust and not be afraid. You *are* my God.

> GOD: I will strengthen you, I will surely help you; I will hold you with my righteous strong hand.

> ME: Yes, Lord! You are my strength. Do help me, Lord, and hold me and never let me go.

This kind of conversational prayer, which draws its words from scripture, is referred to as praying the scriptures. It is a common spiritual practice that brings me peace and calms my fears, as it has done for generations of people.

David, Israel's best-known king, wrote or inspired many of

the Psalms we find in the Bible. A poet and a warrior, he often found his life in danger. His predecessor, King Saul, sought to kill him when David was just a young man. Later, David repeatedly faced challengers to his throne. His fears were not imagined. These were real enemies who wanted his throne, and many of them threatened his very life and the lives of his family. David's response in those times when he was afraid was to compose and sing psalms to God. When he sang about his trust in God, and when he wrote about it, he felt peace. Try reading aloud, or at least whispering, these words of David:

> *Whenever I'm afraid,*
> *I put my trust in you—*
> *in God, whose word I praise.*
> *I trust in God; I won't be afraid.*
> *What can mere flesh [people] do to me?*
>
> (PSALM 56:3–4)

When I was sixteen, I traveled to Mexico City with my high school Spanish class. One evening I went out for a walk by myself (against the rules) and soon lost my bearings in a sprawling metropolis of nearly twenty million people. These were the days long before cell phones. We had just checked into our hotel earlier that day, and for the life of me, I could not remember the name of the hotel, nor where it was located. I walked through the streets of downtown Mexico City that night, increasingly anxious. Then I began to sing hymns to God and I felt a peace come over me. I kept singing until suddenly, to my surprise, I found myself walking down a familiar block. There I was, back at my hotel. I had sung my way from lost to found.

When I'm present with people as they are dying, I can feel their fear. Sometimes, it's just the two of us—the one who is passing and me—though often there are family members by the bedside as well. I anoint the forehead of the dying with oil in the sign of the cross. I share scripture with them, then hold their hands and pray with them, entrusting their lives to God. We'll say the Lord's Prayer together. And then often I will sing hymns to them. In the midst of praying and singing, you can feel their anxiety fade away.

So much of our fear is the result of our hyperactive imagination. Using our amygdala or some other part of our brain, we imagine the threats, dangers, risks, or obstacles as much greater than they really are—as giants in our Promised Land. But I've found that our imagination can also be put to work in visualizing good outcomes and God's deliverance. So instead of imagining that I'll die of cancer, or that the future is grim, or that another 9/11-style attack is looming, I use that same creative power to picture that there is a God—a God who loves me, is with me, and will sustain, strengthen, and carry me. For those facing death, I can help them trust that God is holding them close and to imagine what heaven might be like.

MAYBELLE'S THUNDERSHIRT

My little dog Maybelle is terrified of thunder and fireworks. She doesn't understand these frighteningly loud noises. She doesn't know they cannot hurt her so long as she is inside the house with us. When she hears the rumble and boom, she tries to hide as far away from the sounds as she can get—often under a bed in our basement. I was writing this chapter on a warm June night at the Lake of the Ozarks in central Missouri. We had thunderstorms early in the evening and once the storms cleared, neighbors began shooting off booming fireworks (fireworks are legal at the lake and people set them off all summer long). I'd not been paying attention during the thunderstorm, but once the fireworks began I realized I hadn't seen Maybelle for some time. I found her under a bed, shaking with fear.

There are two things that calm Maybelle when she's afraid of these terrifying noises. The first is to be held snugly in our arms. The second is something called a ThunderShirt, a vest that wraps around her neck and chest and then gets Velcroed tightly around her. It has the same effect on a dog that "swaddling" has on an infant—the dog feels safe, as though she were being held. When my wife first bought the ThunderShirt, I was skeptical. "There is no way this thing will work," I told her. But to my surprise, it does. When Maybelle is terrified of things she doesn't understand—things that are not really a threat to her but which she thinks are a threat—the act of being held, or being wrapped in a shirt that makes her feel like she is being held, takes away her fears and gives her peace. That is the effect faith in God, prayer, reading scripture, singing hymns, and meditating upon God's power, presence, and love has on so many people—it calms the anxious soul.

Saint Paul described the human version of a ThunderShirt two thousand years ago, when he gave this advice for addressing worry, fear, and anxiety to young Christians:

> *The Lord is near. Don't be anxious about anything; rather, bring up all of your requests to God in your prayers and petitions, along with giving thanks. Then the peace of God that exceeds all understanding will keep your hearts and minds safe in Christ Jesus.*
>
> (PHILIPPIANS 4:5*b*–7)

In that vein, I love how Dorothy Bernard, the prolific silent-film actress, said it: "Courage is fear that has said its prayers."

We can focus our imagination on all the things that might happen, and by inflating the threats or obstacles we face, we turn them into giants. Or we can focus our imagination on the presence of God—through prayer, singing hymns, sharing our struggles with close friends, and other spiritual disciplines—and trust that we will sense his love and mercy holding us near. When we imagine God's presence and power we find we can begin to live with courage and hope.

Part Two

CRIME, RACE, TERRORISM, AND POLITICS

5

We Need a Security System

Facts are our friends.

*—*Jerre Stead, CEO of IHS Markit

You will know the truth, and the truth will set you free.

*—*Jesus (John 8:32)

A FEW YEARS AGO, OUR TEAM CONCLUDED A MISSION trip to South Africa with a visit to a wildlife refuge. We stayed several nights in tents adjacent to watering holes where dozens of species of animals, including giraffes, elephants, zebras, and impalas, would gather to drink. It was awe-inspiring to see this multitude standing around the pools of water at sunrise and sunset.

Some of the animals we watched were quite calm as they drank, but other species were terribly skittish and constantly on alert. If they heard any kind of sound, they jumped back, prepared to run. Particularly fearful were the impalas, beautiful gazelles with V-shaped horns and a distinctive mark on their hindquarters—a patch of brown fur in the shape of the letter *M*.

When I asked our guide why these creatures were so skittish, he said, "That *M* you see on their hindquarters stands for McDonald's. They are the cheeseburger of the food chain here in the wild. They are always on high alert, afraid, because so many animals in the wild would gladly eat them."

Watching the impalas, I concluded that their place on the food chain can't make for a pleasant existence. But as I sat there, I also realized how much the impalas reminded me of humans. Like them, we often live on edge—never quite sure who is friend or foe, or from which direction the next threat is likely to come. But there's a big difference. The predators we fear most are not other species but our fellow human beings.

In a recent Gallup poll, 53 percent of Americans reported that they worry "a great deal" about crime and violence.[*] This was up from just 39 percent two years before, and was the highest level since 2001. What led to this surge in fear about violence and crime? The survey was taken just a few months after a mass shooting in San Bernardino, California, in which fourteen people were killed; perhaps that played a part. (The survey was taken before mass shootings in Orlando and Las Vegas.) A steady stream of television shows that include violent crime may foster the concern. Some attribute the fear to twenty-four-hour news programming and our always-on social media. Others think the wave was a result of fearmongering during the 2016 election season. And there *was* an actual uptick in violent crimes in 2016—perhaps the worry is merited.

HELP FOR SKITTISH TIMES

Like the impalas at the watering hole, we can find ourselves skittish around our fellow human beings. That fear is greatest

---

[*] "In U.S., Concern About Crime Climbs to 15-Year High," Gallup, April 6, 2016, http://www.gallup.com/poll/190475/americans-concern -crime-climbs-year-high.aspx.

when we consider crime and violence, but the underlying dread goes deeper than crime statistics. We tend to fear most our fellow human beings who are different from us—those of other religions, races, or socioeconomic groups. We'll consider this fear in its different manifestations in the next few chapters, but for now I'd like to point out an insight that has helped people who are trying to overcome certain fears. It comes from a treatment approach called cognitive therapy.

Cognitive therapy recognizes that feelings often begin with thoughts, and those thoughts are sometimes distorted, based on inaccurate information, faulty assumptions, overly negative views of oneself or the world, or mistaken beliefs—what some call "stinkin' thinkin'." This kind of thinking leads to worry, fear, anxiety, and a host of other misplaced feelings, which in turn can lead to unhealthy or misdirected actions. Cognitive restructuring is a process that is used to identify faulty thinking or assumptions and replace those thoughts with more accurate information and more positive thinking, which in turn offers relief from the problematic feelings.

There's far more to this method than my summary suggests, but you might have already noticed that it seems to echo the first two words of our acronym: "Face your fears with faith" and "Examine your assumptions in light of the facts."

Jerre Stead, CEO of the global information firm IHS Markit, told me that one of the key leadership principles he operates by is "Facts are our friends." Or as Jesus put it in John 8:32, "You will know the truth, and the truth will set you free." Facts can liberate us from faulty assumptions and in the process free us from fear. Because we live in an era of opinions marketed as truths, one in which irrefutable facts are dismissed as "fake news," the challenge is discerning what is true. Having more access to information than ever before, we simply have to do our homework (and that often includes reading perspectives on both sides of an issue or a debate).

AUTOMATIC THOUGHTS AND KNEE-JERK REACTIONS

Cognitive restructuring, as it relates to fear, begins by carefully unpacking the thought processes and information that create the greatest anxiety for you. These are sometimes referred to as automatic thoughts—the phrases and beliefs that you play and replay in your head—things that you have come to accept as true about yourself, others, and the world. Our automatic thoughts could be true, but they often also include assumptions, generalizations, and knee-jerk reactions. We mentioned earlier the idea of catastrophizing—assuming the worst in a situation. That's another type of thinking that arises from and exacerbates fear. There's also the tendency toward black-and-white, either-or thinking (you are either good or bad, with me or against me). Some of these automatic thoughts happen at a nearly subconscious level.

We do this all the time in the area of politics, making assumptions about people of a different party that may not be true. Some do this when it comes to people of other races or other religions—holding and repeating generalizations. We do this on a more personal level when we interpret others' responses to us. If someone doesn't reply to our tweet, text, or e-mail within a short period of time, we assume they don't like us, are mad at us, or don't care about us anymore. Do you ever struggle with unhelpful automatic thoughts?

When we allow automatic thoughts to run unchecked, it can lead to all kinds of unhealthy outcomes, including fear, worry, and anxiety. It's important to question the rationale or assumptions behind these thoughts and then intentionally retrain our thought processes through what is called controlled thinking.

The therapist using this method starts by instructing you to hold any horrible and frightening thought, story, or truth with a healthy dose of skepticism. The next step is to research and seek to discover if the assumption that has led to your fear or anxiety is actually true. From there you begin to develop a way of reminding yourself that the thought that scares you is not in fact true. Eventually, using this method, you retrain your "stinkin' thinkin'" and conquer your fears. Again, there is far more to controlled thinking (entire books have been written about it), and a therapist can be helpful in fully exploiting this tool. But there are some simple commonsense ways you can begin to use this method to identify and unpack your fears, and to seek out the facts concerning them.

STEPHANY'S FEAR OF CATS

Let's take a seemingly innocuous example. Stephany grew up in a home where her mother was allergic to cats. When little Stephany asked for a kitten, her mother told her that kittens make some people sick. When Stephany persisted, her mother described the symptoms of cat allergies in graphic terms. People with allergies struggle to breathe when a cat is around, her mother said. They can get hives on their face, neck, and chest. Their eyes turn red and itch. For Stephany, the prospect of so much misery ended her kitty dreams, but it also planted in her a deep fear of cats.

When Stephany became an adult, her fear meant she avoided dating men who had cats. She would subtly ask about pets before she determined if she would see someone. What if kissing or touching someone who had a cat made her sick? She ended a close friendship with a roommate who wished to get a cat. Keep in mind, she didn't even know if she was allergic to cats. But to her amygdala, cats posed a threat that had grown into a phobia.

It was only after ending a relationship with a man to whom she was deeply drawn that a therapist helped her see how her mother's words had shaped her fears. Together they researched how many people are actually allergic to cats (about one in ten). They looked at symptoms and treatment, and dispelled some misconceptions about cats left over from Stephany's childhood. Then they added exposure therapy—slowly, Stephany allowed herself to be around cats. To Stephany's surprise, she was not allergic to cats at all, and three years later she bought the kitten she'd wanted when she was a child. Correcting her faulty thinking and working up the courage to test her assumptions set her free.

Let's return to the 53 percent of Americans who worry about crime and violence a great deal (another 26 percent reported worrying about crime and violence "a fair amount," for a total of 79 percent who reported at least "a fair amount" of worry about these things).

WHEN FACTS DIFFER FROM FEARS

Americans routinely report that they believe violent crime is on the rise in the United States. This is easy to understand. We see a great deal of crime—including the occasional mass shooting—twenty-four hours a day on the news; then we watch true-crime television shows and go to violent movies. It would be natural for this exposure to lead us to feel unsafe. But the facts about violent crime are quite different from our fears. Here's a chart developed by the Pew Research Center from Bureau of Justice Statistics that I found interesting:

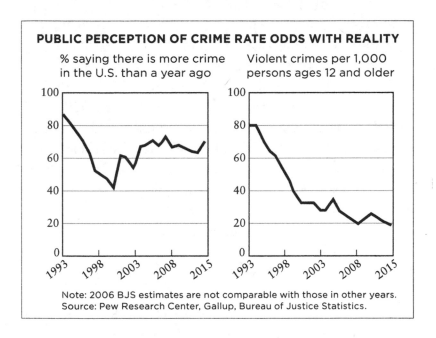

PUBLIC PERCEPTION OF CRIME RATE ODDS WITH REALITY

% saying there is more crime in the U.S. than a year ago

Violent crimes per 1,000 persons ages 12 and older

Note: 2006 BJS estimates are not comparable with those in other years.
Source: Pew Research Center, Gallup, Bureau of Justice Statistics.

Violent crime rates have reduced by more than half since the early 1990s, and the murder rate has dropped to the level it was in 1964. While recent crime rates have risen slightly, they still are down precipitously from their highs of several decades ago. We are *significantly* less likely to be the victims of violent crime than in the early 1990s. In addition, the people most afraid of violent crime—suburbanites—are the least likely to be affected by it. According to the Justice Department, the most likely victim of violent crime is a low-income African American man living in the inner city, and the crimes are often gang-related.

Roughly fifteen thousand murders take place in America

each year, a frightening statistic, particularly when given no context. But consider a recent report in a prominent medical journal estimating that more than 251,000 people die annually in US hospitals due to medical error. This would make medical error the third leading cause of death in the United States.[*] According to this information, you are sixteen times more likely to die as a result of medical error than to be murdered. Even if the study's estimates are radically off and the real number is 125,000, you'd still be eight times more likely to die of medical error than to be murdered. Other data also helps to put violent deaths in perspective. You are twice as likely to die in a car accident in any given year than to be murdered, yet most of us are not afraid every time we get in our car. And for every one person who dies from violent crime each year, forty people will die of heart disease, much of which can be prevented with exercise and diet. Death by heart disease seldom makes the list of top fears in our country.

When we seek out the facts, we often learn that the world is not nearly as scary as we fear. And when it comes to our fear of violent crime, we're much safer than we've been in a generation.

Consider once more our acronym for addressing fear:

Face your fears with faith (trusting that things will work out).
Examine your assumptions in light of the facts.
Attack your anxieties with action.
Release your cares to God.

---

[*] "Study Suggests Medical Errors Now Third Leading Cause of Death in the U.S.," Johns Hopkins Medicine, May 3, 2016, http://www.hopkins medicine.org/news/media/releases/study_suggests_medical_errors_now_ third_leading_cause_of_death_in_the_us.

Exposure focuses on the first and third steps—facing and attacking our fears. Cognitive restructuring is all about the second—examining our assumptions in light of the facts. I'd like to close this chapter by suggesting another spiritual practice that can be very helpful in the fourth step, releasing our fears to God—*lectio divina,* Latin for "divine reading."

LISTENING TO GOD . . . SLOWLY

Lectio divina involves slowing down, reading scripture, meditating upon it, and listening for God to speak to you through the particular passage being considered. Many people read the Bible as though the goal were to finish it as quickly as possible. Each year we present third graders in our church with their first complete Bible. I then encourage them to take six weeks to read the Gospel of Mark (the shortest of the Gospels, and a pretty great place for third graders to start). Inevitably, before the day is out, I have a third grader tell me that she or he has finished reading the entire Gospel. I always commend the child for her or his quick read, but encourage the child to read it again more slowly.

When we're fearful, we can find a great sense of peace by slowing down, meditating upon scripture, and listening for God to speak. Let's take a look at one of the most beautiful passages in the Psalms. King David knew what it was to have enemies seeking to kill him. He'd known such threats throughout his life. But listen to what he wrote:

> *The Lord is my light and my salvation; whom shall I fear?*
> *The Lord is the stronghold of my life; of whom shall I*
> *be afraid? . . . Wait for the Lord; be strong, and let your*
> *heart take courage; wait for the Lord!*
>
> (PSALM 27:1, 14)

It's one thing to read a scripture like this, but it's quite another to trust these words and the God of whom they speak and then to make them your own. When I'm ministering to someone struggling with fear, I find it particularly important to invite the person to read scriptures that speak of confident trust in God in the face of fear. That's why I've included an appendix that provides thirty-one short scripture passages that speak to fear, one for each day of the month. I encourage fearful individuals to start their day by pausing to read and to pray these scriptures. I invite them to do the same at the end of their day. Meditating upon scriptures just before bedtime can have the wonderful impact of calming your fears and helping you to sleep.

The aim of this practice is not to deny the thing you are afraid of or the difficult situation you might find yourself in; rather, it is to be aware of God's presence as you walk through it. I'm reminded of that night in late January 1956 when Dr. Martin Luther King Jr. was leading the Montgomery bus boycott following Rosa Parks's arrest for not giving up her seat on a bus to a white man. The boycott had been going on for weeks. At midnight on January 27, King received a threatening phone call telling him to leave Montgomery if he didn't want to die.

He wrote that he was ready to give up. Weary from the fight, anxious and afraid, he bowed that night at the kitchen table and prayed, confessing his fears and exhaustion to God. It was then that he felt God's presence and heard an inner voice, the voice of the Spirit, saying, "Stand up for righteousness, stand up for truth; and God will be at your side forever." His fears immediately dissipated, and, he noted, "I was ready to face anything."[*]

---

[*] Martin Luther King Jr., *Stride Toward Freedom* (Boston: Beacon Press, 2010), p. 135.

Releasing his fears to God through prayer and meditation led to an awareness of God's presence, and hearing God's voice gave King courage in the face of his fears. I wonder what might have happened to the civil rights movement, or at least King's involvement in it, had he not turned to his faith in that moment.

Though it wasn't *lectio divina* that King practiced that night, it was his persistent reading and meditating upon scripture that shaped his life and gave word to the inner voice he heard calling him to keep going. I'd like to offer you a brief outline of what this kind of meditative reading of scripture looks like.

WHERE TO BEGIN

Begin by finding a quiet place. Start with prayer, something like this: "Lord, I long to hear from you. Speak to me through these words of scripture. I'm listening, Lord." Read the passage slowly and silently to yourself (start with the passages in the appendix, taking one of them each day for a month). Having read the passage once, pray again: "Lord, speak to me; your servant is listening." Then read the scripture aloud, slowly, and see what word or phrase speaks to you. Ponder that word or phrase for a moment. Think about what it means and how it speaks to you and your fears, anxieties, or worries. Pray one final time: "Lord, speak to me; your servant is listening." Now read the passage silently and underline those portions that speak to you. Take these words and incorporate them into your prayers as we learned in chapter 4. For Psalm 27 the prayer might be something like this: "Thank you, Lord, for your presence and love. Please be my light and my salvation. Help me not to be afraid. Help me remember that with you at my side I don't need to be afraid."

We've learned that the truth can set us free, and that, when it comes to addressing fears, facts are our friends. We've also learned that being quiet and listening for God to speak can be a key to overcoming fear. We *can* recover the confident, hope-filled life God intends for us. I'm reminded of the words of Jesus in John 10:10: "The thief enters only to steal, kill, and destroy. I came so that they could have life—indeed, so that they could live life to the fullest."

I began this chapter by describing the scene at a watering hole in Africa, where impalas live in near constant fear of attack. I pointed out that humans are also intricately wired for self-preservation but that, unlike impalas, we tend to fear most others from our own species. Why? We turn next to that question.

oblivious to the racial segregation. I never wondered why there were no black children in either my school or my J. C. Nichols–planned neighborhood. My parents would never have tolerated racial slurs in our home. My teachers at school taught us about civil rights, and many of them saw Dr. King as a hero. They taught us to be proud of our history in Kansas as a free state, about John Brown's raids launched from Kansas into Missouri seeking to overthrow slavery, about the Underground Railroad that ended in Kansas, and about *Brown v. Board of Education of Topeka, Kansas.* Yet, despite all of this, I grew up learning that it was not safe for a white kid like me to venture east of Troost. I don't know who taught me this, but it was an impression that ran deep. Kids like me could be robbed, beaten, or even killed "over there."

TRADING STORIES

Rev. Dr. Emanuel Cleaver III grew up in the same era, just a few years behind me, but on the other side of Troost Avenue. His father is a prominent United Methodist pastor, a former mayor of Kansas City, and now a congressman. We recently sat together over lunch reflecting upon our childhood experiences in the 1980s. Pastor Cleaver told me that sometime during his years growing up he'd picked up that it wasn't safe for black kids to be in the community where I'd been raised. He and his friends thought they could be arrested, beaten, or killed. The perceptions we both had growing up included a fear of the other. I've wondered who had more to fear—a white kid in a mostly black community, or a black kid in a mostly white one?

Both my parents and Dr. Cleaver's were just kids in 1951 when the NAACP sued on behalf of three black children who'd been prevented from buying tickets to swim at the Swope Park

6

Troost Avenue

Cain said to his brother Abel, "Let us go out to the field." And when they were in the field, Cain rose up against his brother Abel, and killed him. Then the Lord said to Cain, "Where is your brother Abel?" He said, "I do not know; am I my brother's keeper?"

—GENESIS 4:8–9

IF YOU WERE TO HONESTLY LIST THE GROUPS OF PEOPLE whom you feel anxious about, how long would your list be, and who would be on it? Most Americans would name terrorist groups like ISIS, but not a small number would go on to name Muslims in general. Some would say that they are afraid of conservatives, while others would say liberals are the real ones we should fear. Undocumented immigrants would be on the list for some and the "alt-right" for others. Persons who are LGBTQ and activists supporting their causes would make the roster for some, while homophobes would register with others. The same goes for atheists on one side and fundamentalist Christians on the other. But the longest-running source of fear of our fellow human beings in America relates to race.

All of us are susceptible to the fear of the other. Politicians, the media, special-interest groups—and sometimes even preachers—raise the specter of people of whom we should be afraid. Fear motivates donors, attracts viewers or hits on social media, and rallies supporters. The prevalence of guns in our country is but one illustration of our fear. Nearly three hundred million guns are stashed in American households, almost one for every man, woman, and child (though those three hundred million guns are owned by less than 40 percent of American households). Many gun owners are hunters who enjoy sport shooting. But the surge in gun ownership in the last few years seems largely to have been fueled by fear. Once again, our brain's fight-or-flight mechanism is a strong motivator to action, especially when paired with a healthy imagination. Unfortunately, when we react out of fear, we too often behave both irrationally and inhumanely toward the people around us.

If someone asked me what groups I feel anxious around or fearful of, I'd say, "I don't think I'm afraid of anyone," and for my best self this would be true. But envy, fear, rivalry, and prejudice tend to be buried deep in all of us.

The story of Cain and Abel has both fascinated and repelled readers for millennia. Scholars believe that the narrative of these two brothers echoes one of the first major divisions in human society—the division between nomadic herdsmen raising livestock by roaming across the land and farmers who settled in stationary places to till the land. The biblical account records God favoring the sacrifices of the herdsman, Abel, over the grain offering of the tiller, Cain. Whatever we make of God's favoring one sacrifice over the other, Cain came to resent and eventually hate his brother until his fear (which I would argue underlies his resentment and hate toward Abel) drove him to murder. Thus begins the story of violence and inhumanity against our fellow humans, even those who live right across the street from us.

THE DIVIDING LINE OF OTHERNESS

Kansas City is a wonderful Midwest metropolis of about two million people. It's also a city whose development was fueled by racial fears and prejudices. In the first half of the twentieth century, a developer named Jesse Clyde Nichols played a huge role in shaping Kansas City (and a host of other planned communities across the United States modeled after his work). He was a brilliant businessman who helped make Kansas City's suburban neighborhoods "livable"—tree-lined streets, large front yards, schools, and convenient shopping districts. But he also instituted *neighborhood covenants* that restricted who could live in these "subdivisions"—this was part of his recipe for building a desirable community.

His development philosophy helped institutionalize the racial biases that were prevalent at that time by prohibiting African Americans from purchasing homes in many of the new—and white—communities. Here's the text of one of those restrictive covenants: "None of the said lots shall be conveyed to, used, owned nor occupied by Negroes as owner or tenants."* In many communities across the United States, including some suburbs in Kansas City, the covenants were expanded to include Jewish people.

The street in Kansas City that serves as the dividing line between predominantly white and black communities is Troost Avenue. I suspect most major cities in America have their own Troost. I grew up in what was then an all-white suburb (it is still predominantly white) called Prairie Village. As a kid, I wa

---

* "'Curse of Covenant' Persists—Restrictive Rules, While Unenforceab
Have Lingering Legacy," *Kansas City Star*, July 27, 2016 (originally p
lished in 2005).

swimming pool in Kansas City. The city claimed that "the policy of operating separate swimming pools for the two races is reinforced by a recognized natural aversion to physical intimacy inherent in the use of swimming pools by members of races that do not mingle socially."* Thurgood Marshall, then chief attorney for the NAACP, argued the case and won. The Swope Park pool would be integrated. In response, the city closed the pool while it awaited an appeal of the case. When the pool finally reopened in 1954, and a few black children came to swim, their parents were afraid for their safety. Later, as an increasing number of black children came to the pool, white parents no longer allowed their children to swim there. Why? Because they were afraid. Fear was present on both sides of the racial divide. Fear is the underlying driver of racial prejudice.

More than a thousand books have been written on segregation and other racially based policies that continue to this day. This book is aimed at inviting us to be unafraid, and to live with courage and hope. How do we overcome racial fear, and the accompanying racism and prejudice, in our communities and within ourselves?

We've learned that many of our fears are irrational and do not reflect reality, and to combat them we must examine the assumptions that lead to our fear of the other. This happens when we get to know the people who live on the other side of our Troost Avenue. It's one thing to read or think about "the other," but something crucial happens when you actually get to know others, particularly as you develop friendships with them.

---

* Laura Ziegler, "Swope Park Pool Desegregation Case Important to Kansas City Civil Rights Struggle," KCUR, February 25, 2016, http://kcur .org/post/swope-park-pool-desegregation-case-important-kansas-city-civil -rights-struggle#stream/0.

Last year, the congregation I serve, which is located six miles west of Troost, and St. James United Methodist Church, located on the east side of the avenue, began plotting: we decided it was time to get to know one another better. In order to do that we thought we would begin with a simple conversation, listening to one another's stories. We gathered hundreds of our members from the two congregations at St. James for a couple of hours of listening, learning, and eating ice cream together. Subsequently, we gathered a large group of members from both churches at the Church of the Resurrection for another evening of learning, listening, and fellowship. Since then we've held joint fellowship events and learning experiences, gatherings in one another's homes, and more as we work together to develop meaningful relationships while we examine our assumptions and attack our anxieties with action.

Todd and his wife, Laura, moved to Kansas City several years ago so that Todd could join our pastoral team at our downtown Kansas City campus. As they were looking for a house for their small family, Todd and Laura made it clear to their real estate agent that they wanted to live in a predominantly African American neighborhood east of Troost. Todd and Laura are white. They were moving from North Carolina, where they had also lived in a predominantly African American community. Their strategy was simple—they wanted to be one small part of breaking down the racial barrier and helping whatever city they live in to look more like the kingdom Jesus proclaimed.

Their own story and the stories they told serve as lessons for the rest of us in how to overcome false events that appear real. Their neighbors welcomed them with open arms. They were protective of Todd and Laura and their children, and wanted to bless them. Todd noted that the parents next door were their heroes, having raised nineteen children, only seven of whom were their biological children; the other twelve were foster or adopted children or simply kids who were in trouble and needed help. In the process of finding their own lives changed by living east of Troost, Todd and Laura were also breaking down barriers in their neighborhood about the folks who typically lived west of Troost.

We've been blessed to have African American pastors who intentionally choose to join our staff at Resurrection, caring for and loving people as a way of tearing down walls and helping our community to examine their assumptions and fears related to those who are racially "the other."

There will be no Troost Avenue in heaven. When we pray "Thy kingdom come, Thy will be done on earth as it is in heaven," that prayer is meant to shape our actions. We're meant not only to pray but to act—my Anglican friends enjoy saying it in Latin: *ora et labora,* pray *and* work. This is especially true, I would add, when you're afraid of the other. We pray for God's kingdom to come on earth, and then we work and live in such a way that we see our community become more like the kingdom of God.

To be courageous means you do what you know is right even when you are afraid. The author of 1 John offers a profound statement to this effect when he writes, "There is no fear in love, but perfect love drives out fear" (4:18). The Greek word for "love" in this verse is *agape,* which signifies not a warm feeling, but actions done with the motivation of blessing and caring for others, even if they come at personal expense. But don't miss what John makes plain for us: the very act of doing what is loving to another has the power to cast fear from *our* lives.

A SIMPLE QUESTION

Jesus preached that the essence of God's hope and expectation for the human race was that we love God with our entire being, and that we love our neighbor as we love ourselves. He even said that we were called to love our enemy. If this ethic of love sounds too high-minded to be of much practical use, we can start by asking one very concrete question: "In the situation I find myself in, what is the most loving thing that I can do?"

It's surprising how often this simple question helps us to make the right decision, particularly when we're afraid. By the way, when God questioned Cain concerning the whereabouts of his brother Abel, after Cain had killed him, Cain's response to God was, "Am I my brother's keeper?" Cain asked an interesting question, but what he did not seem to grasp is that to God the answer is "Yes, you *are* your brother's keeper."

I don't know what your community's Troost Avenue is, and who lives on the other side of it from you. Your divide may be between Hispanic and Caucasian people, gay and straight, rich and poor, conservative and liberal. The failure to get to know our neighbors, and the shirking of our responsibility to love them, means that we will continue to live with fear. But love perfected by actions has the power to drive out fear.

7

Weaponizing Fear

They want you to be full of fear. Of them. All the time. . . . And they'll do just about anything to try and make that happen.

—SANDEE LaMOTTE, CNN correspondent

We're not born to hate. We're born to want to be nurtured and valued and loved and to give love.

—MINDY CORPORON, whose son and father were gunned down outside the Jewish Community Center of Greater Kansas City, Overland Park, Kansas, April 13, 2014

SINCE THAT TERRIBLE MORNING IN SEPTEMBER 2001, terrorism has been part of our collective psyche. It's not that this was the first taste of terrorism for Americans, but on that day those of us old enough to remember witnessed the unthinkable—something so inconceivably grotesque that we watched it over and over again on television trying to wrap our minds around what we had just seen. All these years later I can't watch footage of the planes flying into the World Trade Center without tearing up. These coordinated attacks did exactly what al-Qaeda hoped for—they struck fear in the heart of not only America but much of the world.

TERROR IN THE MEGAPHONE

This is, of course, the point of terrorism—to make others afraid. At least that's the terrorists' starting point. Terrorism allows groups with relatively small numbers of people to gain notoriety for their cause and to have influence beyond their actual power. And in our digital age this means doing the most outrageous things possible in order to get the maximum news coverage, allowing a single relatively small act, carried out by one or two or three people, to be heard and seen around the world. As CNN correspondent Sandee LaMotte puts it, "They want you to be full of fear. Of them. All the time. . . . And they'll do just about anything to try and make that happen."

Most Westerners don't understand why a suicidal movement that kills civilians could have such wide appeal. According to interviews with former ISIS fighters, some were drawn to the group as a protest movement against what they saw as the tyranny of various world powers or the perceived oppression of Muslims. For others, it was the appeal of establishing an Islamic caliphate—a kingdom for faithful Muslims that transcends all national boundaries. Some see the movement as ushering in an Islamic vision of the End Times.

Interestingly, many in the Islamic world believe that ISIS was the creation of the United States and Western powers, aimed at destabilizing the Middle East and turning Muslims against one another. When I first heard this from a military expert on ISIS, I found it hard to believe. And then I traveled to Egypt. While sitting and talking to Egyptians, I learned that this is precisely what they believe about ISIS.

The perception that most of us have in America is that ISIS has as its primary focus killing Americans and Europeans. Yet in the first half of 2017, only 1.7 percent of the 1,670 people killed by ISIS were European or American (29 persons), while more than 95 percent of their victims were Muslims living in Islamic countries.* While I reject the idea that the United States directly helped to create ISIS, I do believe our views of this terrorist organization and its connection to the broader Islamic community are skewed.

Today, thanks to various terrorist groups, including al-Qaeda and ISIS, and their effective use of the media as a megaphone broadcasting their outrageous acts, Americans and others in the West find themselves increasingly fearful, not only of these extremist groups but, more broadly, of Muslims as a whole. Fear so easily turns to hate. As I wrote these words an improvised explosive device was detonated outside a mosque in Minnesota as Muslims were beginning to gather for morning prayer. In this case, fear led the bomber to become the very monster he or she hates—a violent terrorist.

In our conversation about how to find a more courageous, hopeful way of living in uncertain times, we need to look squarely at the terrorist giant. Who are these people and groups we've become so fearful of? Have we magnified the threat? Do we have the resources to differentiate between friend and foe? Under the stress of fear, have we neglected to examine our assumptions in light of the facts? Are we in danger of becoming the very thing we hate? And what practical steps can we take to find a way forward? Tragically, almost every community around the globe has its own story to tell here. With your permission, I'd like to start with mine.

---

* https://storymaps.esri.com/stories/terrorist-attacks/?year=2017. The data here is crowdsourced and offers a report of both attacks and fatalities.

WHAT THE MUSLIM NEIGHBORS SAID

Several Islamic centers have been built in Kansas City in the last ten years. A new and relatively large one was recently built near the church I pastor. During the construction, I heard from several people in the community who *had heard from someone, who had heard from someone else, who had read something online* about these Islamic centers in our city being bases for radicalizing Muslims. In an environment where people are already afraid, these kinds of innuendos, comments, and fears find fertile ground to take root and spread without anyone taking the time to discover the truth, or to meet or get to know people from other communities.

I had a chance to sit down and talk with a couple of leaders from the Islamic center. They told me about their lives, families, and faith. One was a respected physician, another a respected business leader. They voiced their utter disdain for terrorism and those who commit murderous acts in the name of their faith. In their eyes, the terrorists were not true Muslims. They asked if they could worship with us one Sunday. When they did, I introduced them and their families to the congregation. Members of my congregation went to Friday prayers at their mosque, both to understand who our Muslim neighbors are and to express their concern for their well-being.

As we've already learned, something happens when you actually get to know people you might otherwise have been afraid of. More often than not, your fears disappear and your suspicions fade. You find you have empathy and compassion for them. Ideally, you make new friends. I see our story with our Muslim neighbors as an example of ordinary people facing their fears with faith, examining their assumptions in light of the facts, and attacking their fears with action. The result?

Compassion and concern replaced suspicion and fear. All of us were less afraid.

Looking at the facts can help us to address our fears about Muslims. Do some Muslims commit grievous acts? Of course, as do some Christians. But with 1.5 billion Muslims in the world, it is worth asking how many people have been killed by Islamic terror on US soil in the years since 9/11. The answer is, as of the writing of this book, 94. Since 9/11 there have been ten terrorist attacks on US soil that killed one or more people, including the Pulse nightclub shooting in June 2016, where 49 of the 94 who have died since 9/11 perished. These 94 deaths were tragic and horrible losses, but the facts demonstrate that they are one category of tragic loss among many. By comparison, during those same sixteen years when 94 died at the hands of terrorists, 9,600 people died in the United States by lightning strike, more than 160,000 died from murders unrelated to terrorism, and 560,000 died in automobile accidents. You are statistically 120 times more likely to be struck by lightning each year in the United States than to be killed by an Islamic terrorist. You are 2,000 times more likely to be murdered by an American who is not an Islamic terrorist. You are 7,000 times more likely to die in a car accident.

None of this means we should not be concerned about terrorism. I'm grateful for all the civil servants and elected officials who work so hard to prevent future attacks. My point is not to minimize their work—it is critically important and has played a key part in preventing further assaults against our country. My point is that, as with so many other things, our fears of Islamic terrorism are out of proportion to the actual threat, and these fears may lead us to act in ways that are inappropriate and even harmful to others, including our Muslim neighbors.

I've spoken with many people in my community who, in the

face of the debate over whether the United States should receive Syrian refugees, were fearful of our country accepting these displaced persons, particularly if they were to move to Kansas City. I asked them if they could recall any terrorist attacks committed by Muslims in Kansas City since 2001. (There have been no such incidents.)

"WE'RE NOT BORN TO HATE"

Kansas City has, however, suffered another form of terrorism: several racially or religiously motivated hate crimes. In one case, the violence was aimed at the Jewish community. Frazier Glenn Miller, a former member of the KKK, came to Kansas City on Palm Sunday in 2014 with the intention of killing Jewish people. He drove to the Jewish Community Center near the Church of the Resurrection and shot and killed Dr. Bill Corporon and his grandson Reat Underwood, as Bill was taking Reat to tryouts for a talent contest. Both were members of the congregation I pastor. Miller then drove to a care center for the elderly, run by the Jewish community, and killed Terri LaManno as she was getting out of her car to visit her mother, who was a resident of the care center. A Roman Catholic, Terri was the aunt of one of my staff members.

Mindy Corporon, whose father and son were killed that day, responded to this act of terror and evil not by living a life of fear, but by devoting her life to combating racial and religious misunderstanding and hatred and working to bring people of different faiths and ethnic backgrounds together. "We're not born to hate," says Mindy. "We're born to want to be nurtured and valued and loved and to give love." She's one of the most amazing women I know, and an inspiring example for the rest of us about what it means to attack or address our fear with actions.

In 2016, a second hate crime occurred not far from the Church of the Resurrection. On this occasion, another white man, Adam Purinton, came to a neighborhood bar and grill and hurled insults at two Indian men, who were both engineers. "Get out of my country," he told them. He was asked to leave but returned thirty minutes later and killed one of the men, Srinivas Kuchibhotla, and injured two others in the bar. Later he would tell a friend he was on the run, having just killed two "Iranian people."

A third hate crime occurred when a Somali man who identified as a Christian, Ahmed Aden, intentionally ran over and killed a Muslim, a fifteen-year-old Somali American named Abdisamad Sheikh-Hussein, as he was leaving his mosque. The bumper sticker on Aden's SUV read "Quran is a virus disease (worse) than Ebola."

These represent a very small number of hate crimes relative to the Kansas City population. Note, however, that none of these hate crimes was carried out by Islamic terrorists, but rather by people who had some connection to the Christian faith, albeit a twisted version of it.

FEARING AN ENEMY WE DON'T UNDERSTAND

Many Christians today look upon the world's 1.5 billion Muslims with fear. This fear is not new; it goes back to the struggle between Islam and Christianity starting in the seventh century. In addition to the past conflicts and wars, our natural "impala instinct" leaves us uncertain and cautious about people who don't dress the way we do, share our beliefs, or look like us.

The 9/11 attacks left a deep scar on our collective psyche and a fear of an enemy we do not understand. This enemy associates itself with Islam in much the same way the KKK was linked to Christianity. That scar is reinforced by every act of violence perpetrated or inspired by ISIS. And because most of us know so little about the Islamic faith or the history of the Middle East, we are ill equipped to differentiate between the radical beliefs of ISIS and the Islam of our Muslim neighbors.

Giving in to fear of all Muslims by isolating them and treating them with suspicion or contempt only serves the cause of the terrorist who hopes to force just such a response. Our Muslim neighbors need our understanding that the difference between the Islam they practice and that of ISIS is as vast as the difference between Frazier Glenn Miller's Christianity and the faith of most American Christians.

How do we overcome this form of fear of the other? I think it requires the courage to befriend our Muslim neighbors, to get to know them, and to better understand their faith. We have to inform ourselves about the relative magnitude of the threat posed by the radical forms of Islam. And we have to choose to meet the threat of hate on the part of a very small group with the power of love for the vast majority of Muslims.

As Dr. King famously noted, hate will never defeat hate—only love is capable of doing that, the perfect love that casts out all fear. This is the love of neighbor (and love of enemy) that Jesus demands of us.

History shows that when America acts out of fear instead of courage and compassion, we almost always do the wrong thing. I'm reminded of Franklin Delano Roosevelt's first inaugural address, given at a time when the Depression was at its worst—with 25 percent of the population unemployed. You remember his famous line: "The only thing we have to fear is fear itself—nameless, unreasoning, unjustified terror which paralyzes needed efforts to convert retreat into advance." But in 1942, not long after the attack on Pearl Harbor, American fear of the Japanese was so great that this same president issued an executive order to forcibly relocate over one hundred thousand people of Japanese ancestry—most of them American citizens—from the nation's coasts to internment camps in an attempt to calm the fears of other Americans. Japanese Americans needed the president to lead with moral courage, but his courage failed him and them.

AN INDEFINITELY SUSPENDED WELCOME

Sadly, we can count on more acts of terrorism in the years ahead—those who would use violence to further their agenda will not stop, and our intelligence and law enforcement agencies will need to remain vigilant and constantly devise new methods for fending off such attacks. And it is likely that at some point we will fail to prevent an assault. But the greater failure would be the loss of our courage, our compassion, and our willingness to welcome the stranger in distress and to love our neighbor as we love ourselves. In the face of a major humanitarian crisis related to refugees, I'm reminded of God's word to his people through the prophet Jeremiah: "The LORD proclaims: Do what is just and right; rescue the oppressed from the power of the oppressor. Don't exploit or mistreat the refugee, the orphan, and the widow" (Jeremiah 22:3).

The greatest humanitarian crisis in the world today is taking place in Syria. Millions have fled the country. We've resettled some Syrian refugees in our country, though recently we indefinitely suspended welcoming such persons—a decision that left some Americans feeling safer. Members of my own congregation were divided over this decision. In response to it, I sat down with a Syrian refugee family that had resettled in Kansas City before the ban went into effect. In the family's living room, I listened as the husband and wife told their story while their children sat quietly on the couch.

They described their daughter's life-threatening medical condition that ultimately allowed them to resettle in the United States. I asked about the circumstances in their hometown in Syria, where the husband had worked at an auto-body shop. They told me that the power had been off in their town for the last three months, even as the population swelled with refugees. People were burning furniture and whatever else they could find to stay warm in the winter. When the medical treatment their daughter needed was no longer available, they decided they had to leave. When I asked them to describe the day they left, they began to weep. This man and his wife had left behind everything they owned, along with their aging parents, siblings, friends, and the land they loved, in order to save their daughter's life. They said that they would never forget the sadness of leaving their home. After two years in refugee camps, they were able to begin a new life in the United States.

GRANT US COURAGE

I left my visit grateful for the people, many of them Jewish and Christian, who had provided for this family and befriended them so that they could start over. I believe both our government's decision to allow them in and the welcome extended by many in Kansas City were efforts to overcome fear with courage and compassion.

As I was writing this chapter I found myself humming the second verse of Harry Emerson Fosdick's famous hymn "God of Grace and God of Glory." He penned these words in 1930, in the depths of the Great Depression, when the world appeared to be sliding toward yet another world war. The refrain is a prayer that concludes,

Grant us wisdom, grant us courage,
for the living of these days.

Living with courage comes in part as we face our fears with faith, examine our assumptions in light of facts, attack our anxieties with action, and release our cares to God, praying for his wisdom, strength, and peace.

Among the many questions we wrestle with as a nation and as individuals today is this: what must we do to keep our nation safe, while at the same time demonstrating courageous compassion for those fleeing oppression in their lands? We may not see eye to eye on how we balance security and compassion, but I pray that our response both to our Muslim neighbors and to the Muslim refugees from war-torn countries will reflect our values and the ideals of our nation—that we might continue to be the land of the free and the home of the brave.

8

The Sky Is Falling!

God is our refuge and strength, a help always near in times of great trouble.
That's why we won't be afraid when the world falls apart.
—Psalm 46:1–2a

WHEN I WAS FOUR OR FIVE, MY PARENTS READ ME A little book called *Henny Penny*. The fact that I still remember the name, the story, and the refrain all these years later tells me it must have left a great impression on me. While this book came out in 1968, the story has been told for at least 2,500 years and is known more commonly as the tale of Chicken Little. Its earliest known telling follows a rabbit who believes the world is collapsing. It was told by the Buddha. In every age, human beings have struggled with fear.

In the version I read growing up, a hen named Henny Penny is scratching at the ground one day when an acorn falls on her head. Startled, she declares, "The sky is FALLING!" and runs off to tell the king. Along the way she meets her friends—a rooster, a goose, a duck, and a turkey—and she tells each one that the sky is falling. Each in turn is seized by fear, and a kind of animal hysteria breaks loose. The point of the story is to show how easy it is to catastrophize what's happening around us, and how quickly this kind of fear can spread when we pass it on to others.

If you read the story as a child, you'll recall that fear led these poor animals to suspend their logic. On the way to tell the king the news, they meet a red fox, who offers to show them a shortcut to the palace. Their fear has kept them from seeing straight and recognizing the fox as their predator. They follow the fox right into his den where they become dinner for the fox's family.

We live in a time when it feels like the sky is falling. I was struck by Molly Ball's comment, quoted in chapter 1: "Fear is in the air, and fear is surging. Americans are more afraid today than they have been in a long time." As you may recall, when I surveyed the Resurrection congregation about their fears, the top concern of those over age fifty was "fear for the direction of our country." It is to that fear we turn now.

THE SIMPLEST EMOTION TO TWEAK

One of the reasons I dread election seasons is that so much of the rhetoric and the advertising aims to conjure up fear in people. The strategy is so obvious it's embarrassing. Rick Wilson, a Republican political strategist and media consultant, notes, "Fear is the simplest emotion to tweak in a campaign ad. You associate your opponent with terror, with fear, with crime, with causing pain and uncertainty."* Is this the recipe for increasing your chances of winning an election? Sadly, in many cases the answer is yes. When people become afraid, they are more motivated to get to the polls.

It's not just politicians who play to our fears. Dr. Shana Gadarian, who teaches political science at Syracuse University

---

* Quoted in Molly Ball, "Donald Trump and the Politics of Fear," *The Atlantic*, September 2, 2016.

and is the coauthor of *Anxious Politics: Democratic Citizenship in a Threatening World,* found that when people are anxious, they tend to seek out information from sources that actually reinforce their anxiety. We can see footage from the latest terrorist act over and over and over again on twenty-four-hour news. We don't tend to look for the sources that say "the chances of this happening in your community are one in 3.6 billion."

Many of us turn to the same news outlet day after day, and our views become largely shaped by that particular source, whether it's Facebook, Twitter, the *New York Times,* CNN, Fox News, or the *Drudge Report.* With this in mind, you might consider taking a different tack. For example, I've found it helpful to tune in to multiple news sources to try to understand the perspective of others. I read the *New York Times* and watch Fox News. I read *Slate* and Breitbart News. I don't necessarily read each of these because I agree with their points of view—some hold views the opposite of my own. I read them because I want to understand how others are thinking, what they are feeling, what they fear, and what they propose.

"LEFT" AND "RIGHT" IN JESUS'S INNER CIRCLE

Recently, I was visiting with a friend, Glen Miles, the senior pastor of First Community Church of Columbus, Ohio. We were talking about the divide in our country and the fears on both sides of that divide. He reminded me that the men Jesus called to be his disciples represented a spectrum of likely hostile points of view. Matthew was a tax collector working for the Romans and by that work supporting their rule over Palestine. Simon the Zealot, as his name makes clear, was a member of the Zealots, a political party committed to the overthrow of the Romans and all who collaborated with them. These two men were as far apart politically as you could be in first-century Palestine, yet Jesus called both to follow him. I wonder what kind of mealtime discussions these two disciples had. I wonder if they saw their political views change during the three years they sat under Jesus's teaching.

When someone asks me, "Are you liberal or conservative?," my response is always "Yes, of course." If the questioner then asks, "No, which one are you?," my response is "Both. I'm liberal on some things, conservative on others." I suspect the same is true for many of you reading this book. To be liberal means, in the best sense, to be open to new ideas, open to reform, respectful of individual rights, and generous. To be conservative, in the best sense, means to hold to traditional values and ideas, exercising appropriate caution when faced with change. If we are liberal without any conserving impulse, we become unmoored, jettisoning important truths and values simply because they are old. (I'm reminded of something a professor once said to me: "All that is old may not be gold, but all that is new may not be true.") If we are conservative without a liberal impulse, we become intransigent, unwilling to reform or embrace change. I find the ability to listen to people on both sides of national political debates (as well as both sides of theological debates within Christianity) helps me not to give in to the "sky is falling" mind-set, for often each side believes the sky is falling for opposite reasons.

I recall after President Obama's reelection one of my friends said he was so discouraged and so afraid for the future of our country that he stood out in the yard that night and wept. Some of my other friends celebrated with great enthusiasm. Four years later, on the night that President Trump was elected, I spoke to two different young women who were in tears, deeply distraught by his election and afraid for the future of our country. Others I know and care about were celebrating.

When it comes to the fears we feel related to the direction of our country, our acronym for overcoming fear is particularly helpful:

Face your fears with faith.
Examine your assumptions in light of the facts.
Attack your anxieties with action.
Release your cares to God.

Americans have good reason to have faith in the resiliency of our country and the efficacy of our system of checks and balances. We've survived some very interesting characters in the White House over the course of our history. Ultimately, though, the bedrock of faith is not in our country but in the God who rules over all things. I love these words of the psalmist, and I turn to them often during difficult times:

> God is our refuge and strength, a help always near in
>   times of great trouble.
> That's why we won't be afraid when the world falls
>   apart. . . .
> Nations roar; kingdoms crumble.
> God utters his voice; the earth melts.
> The Lord of heavenly forces is with us!
> The God of Jacob is our place of safety.
>
>   (PSALM 46:1–2a, 6–7)

A HELP ALWAYS NEAR

In addition to facing our fears with faith, we can examine our assumptions in light of the facts. I'm skeptical that anyone can tell the whole truth in a sixty-second campaign commercial or a canned debate response. I will fact-check when candidates and their campaigns seek to persuade me with fear. I will do my best to listen to and understand both sides of the argument.

If we feel anxious about a candidate or an issue, we should get involved—working to address the issue behind our fears can help dissipate the anxiety. But if we choose to act, we must do so in a way that reflects our character and faith. We don't need more people playing the part of Chicken Little or Henny Penny, proclaiming the sky is falling, spreading hysteria, or catastrophizing the state of our country or world. Because we all struggle with worry, fear, anxiety, and the tendency to catastrophize, the Chicken Little syndrome can be found among conservatives and progressives, the right and the left, Republicans and Democrats.

The further we move toward the extremes of the ideological divide, the more fear, worry, and anxiety seem to inform and control assumptions, and consequently the positions that are advocated. Fear gives way to paranoia and hate. We've seen this demonstrated in many of the groups now referred to as the alt-right (the alternative right). Anti-Semitism, white nationalism, white supremacy, and the KKK reflect various impulses in the most "alt" of the alt-right. They fear the loss of white identity and culture. They decry multiculturalism, mixed races, the idea of the "melting pot" of American culture. They are concerned that their heritage and cultures are being "erased."

That fear, and many other fears, drive them to hate and often to violence.

The far left, though fewer in number, share some traits with the alt-right. They also tend to see the world in black-and-white terms and to catastrophize. And at the extreme of the far left, some individuals and groups are willing to use violence in an attempt to silence the haters on the right. But doesn't that choice ultimately undermine their cause and the moral authority they might otherwise have?

Most Americans don't identify with either of the extremes. The extremes are seen as fringe groups, though in the aftermath of President Trump's election the alt-right was emboldened. In the face of ever more strident voices from the left and right, it is important to, in the words of Proverbs 31:8, "speak out on behalf of the voiceless, and for the rights of all who are vulnerable." And it is important to do so in a way that doesn't stoop to the level of the extremists. Jesus calls his followers to love their enemies and to pray for those who persecute them. He believed, and demonstrated, the power of love to conquer one's enemies.

Saint Paul's strategy for dealing with those who wrong you, drawn from Proverbs 25:21–22, was as follows:

If possible, to the best of your ability, live at peace with all people. Don't try to get revenge for yourselves, my dear friends, but leave room for God's wrath. It is written, Revenge belongs to me; I will pay it back, says the Lord. *Instead,* If your enemy is hungry, feed him; if he is thirsty, give him a drink. By doing this, you will pile burning coals of fire upon his head. *Don't be defeated by evil, but defeat evil with good.*

(ROMANS 12:18–21)

How we treat those with whom we disagree is a both a test and a demonstration of our character and faith. Being right is not the defining mark of the Christian life. We are defined—and ultimately judged—by how we practice love.

We must speak up, stand up, and work for what is right and just. But when we've done all we can in pursuit of what is right as we understand right, we have to release our concerns to God. I don't believe God dictates the outcome of elections, or is pushing buttons and pulling strings in our national politics. God allows individuals and nations to do foolish and sometimes evil things that are the opposite of his will. But God has a way of working through the evil around us and those who participate in it or advocate for it. God specializes in forcing good from evil, of bending the foolishness of humans to accomplish a higher purpose. Trusting this helps me to feel hopeful about the future of our nation.

No, Henny Penny, the sky is not falling. God is our refuge and strength, a help always near in times of great trouble. That's why we don't have to be afraid, even when the world seems to be falling apart.

Part Three

FAILURE, DISAPPOINTING OTHERS, INSIGNIFICANCE, AND LONELINESS

9

"But What If I Fail?"

Success consists of going from failure to failure without loss of enthusiasm.

—ATTRIBUTED TO WINSTON CHURCHILL

A FRIEND SUGGESTED I WRITE A BOOK ABOUT FEAR. HE was forty-seven years old at the time and had recently made a major career change. This strong, talented guy had left behind a good job to look for new challenges and new opportunities. He lives on the West Coast. When we talked, he'd just accepted a job in New York City.

He told me that one day, as he was walking down a street in midtown Manhattan—his wife and children nearly three thousand miles away—doubts began to creep into his thoughts. What was he doing here? How could he be asking his family to make such a huge change? What if he failed? Before long, fear and anguish had overwhelmed him. As he walked through the city—skyscrapers towering on either side, strangers by the hundreds streaming past—anxiety welled up in his heart, and tears welled up in his eyes.

Then a slight shift in perspective happened. He told me, "I began to look around at all of these people quickly passing me by, and I wondered how many of these thousands of people also struggle with fear of failure. It struck me that likely all of them, at times, were afraid. I began to feel a certain comfort in the universality of fear. I was not alone in my fear."

The fear of failure—along with all the awful accompanying scenarios we imagine of shame, the inability to provide for ourselves and those we love, and the stigma of losing—is one of the most prevalent of human fears. In our congregational survey, it loomed as the number one fear for those under fifty (and still tied for fourth among those over fifty). A culture that makes success or at least the appearance of it the only option for everyone, starting in childhood, exacts a steep cost: if you don't succeed, you're often left feeling that you are a loser—a nobody. In this and the next few chapters we'll look at failure and other kinds of deep personal fears that lurk just out of sight for almost everyone.

"THIS IS DOOMED TO FAIL"

Twenty-seven years ago, I was assigned by the United Methodist bishop of Missouri to start a new congregation on the south side of Kansas City. We began with just a handful of people. Several pastors had already warned me that the project was underfunded and likely to fail. One pastor even said to me, "This is doomed to fail, and when it does it will be a black mark on your career. It will really set you back. Just tell them you don't want to do this; they'll find a better position for you in an existing church." What encouragement! The failure rate for new church starts at the time was 50 percent. Questions swirled in my mind? Would anyone show up for our first worship service? Did I have what it takes to successfully develop a congregation from nothing? We had funds to last for eight months, after which my income would be cut significantly, and I had an infant and a three-year-old daughter. *What will happen to my family if this church fails?*

Today, even though that little congregation is now quite large, fears of failure occasionally creep back into my thoughts and feelings. These days it's more like a twist in the pit of my stomach, telling me that the change we're making, or the new initiative we're pursuing, or the controversial sermon I'll be offering will most certainly fail.

Do you ever fear failure? What kind of impending personal defeat keeps you awake at night? In the past, when the voice in your head said that you should give up, what did you do? Did you take the risk and keep going, or turn back while you still could?

TO LIVE IS TO RISK

In Luke's Gospel, Jesus spoke of "counting the cost." We must practice wise discernment as we seek to pursue a path that requires risk taking. I tend to ask questions like these: "Am I sure this is the right thing to do?" "What are the likely outcomes, both good and bad?" "Does the good accomplished justify the risk taken?" But here's an important life lesson—to live is to risk. If you always choose the risk-free, completely safe, and convenient path in life, you'll find the failure you experience is the failure to truly live.

J. K. Rowling, whose Harry Potter books have sold more than four hundred million copies, saw her first manuscript rejected by twelve different publishing houses before one picked it up, paying an advance of £1,500—less than $3,000. Even then her editor told her she needed to get a day job because she'd never really be able to support herself selling children's books.

In her magnificent 2008 Harvard commencement address she recalled, "What I feared most for myself at your age was not poverty, but failure." She described her own failure, which climaxed in her being divorced and jobless, struggling to raise a daughter on her own. But persistence in spite of her fears laid the foundation for her eventual success. Rowling noted, "It is impossible to live without failing at something, unless you live so cautiously that you might as well not have lived at all—in which case, you fail by default."

I love stories like Rowling's. They remind us that failure isn't the end and is often essential for becoming the person and achieving the goals of your dreams.

In chapter three we read about the Israelites being paralyzed by fear a mile from the promised land. But forty-two years earlier Moses stood paralyzed before a burning bush in the middle of the Sinai. At the time, the Israelites were still slaves in Egypt. He heard the voice of God calling him to go to Egypt to confront Pharaoh and to demand the release of the slaves. Moses was eighty years old. For forty years he had lived in the Sinai wilderness tending his father-in-law's sheep, a fugitive who had fled Egypt after killing an Egyptian taskmaster. There was no way he was going back to demand that Pharaoh liberate the Israelite slaves.

As God called Moses to go, Moses began making excuses. Four times he offered a challenge, a roadblock, or an excuse to avoid God's call. Four times God responded, addressing Moses's concerns. Finally, an exasperated and fearful Moses cried out, "Please, my Lord, just send someone else."

I understand. More than once in my life I have felt called to do something that was clearly the right thing to do, but I made excuses to God or to my conscience or to other people. Why? Because I felt anxious, certain I couldn't do it, clear that it would be too hard, convinced I would fail. What I wanted most at those times was for God to send someone else.

Can you relate? I've learned and benefited from some principles over the last twenty-eight years related to the fear of failure that you might find helpful too.

The first is that *most things are never as hard as you fear they will be*. And even if you do fail at them, the pain almost never ends up being as painful as you worry it will be. When you "just do it," you often find yourself surprised at what you can accomplish.

The second is something I learned twenty years ago in a time management course: "Successful people [however you define success] are willing to do the things that unsuccessful people are unwilling to do."* Fear keeps many people and organizations from ever achieving their real potential.

And the third principle, which I've shared with many leaders over the years, I call "discernment by nausea."** Often when you come to a fork in the road, a decision you have to make between taking this path or another, you'll find that one path seems easier, safer, and more convenient. More often than not, though, the other path—the one that's harder, riskier, more inconvenient, the one that leaves you feeling a bit nauseous when you think about it—is the one you should take. Jesus used different language to comment on the same phenomenon. He noted that life tends to present us with two roads we could take. One is broad and easy, yet it leads to destruction. The other is narrow and hard, but it leads to life.

---

* I'm not sure who originally said this, but it was quoted in the Franklin time management course I took in the early 1990s and I've never forgotten it.

** I believe this term is original with me—I've been sharing it with leaders for over twenty years. Apologies if someone else said it first.

SEEING BEYOND THE END OF THE ROAD

We're all afraid of failing. As we've seen, a critical function of our amygdala is to keep us safe and reduce risk. It does this by identifying threats, which our fertile imaginations then spin into a torrent of worst possible scenarios. Yet this very system meant to protect us can also keep us from really living. Some risks are meant to be taken. I love hockey legend Wayne Gretzky's famous quote: "You miss 100% of the shots you don't take." Failure can be painful, yet nearly every rewarding thing that we'll experience or do in life comes with the chance that we might fail.

One of my favorite television commercials of all time is the 1997 Nike spot for Air Jordan XII tennis shoes. The spot was called "Failure," and featured Michael Jordan walking down a corridor as we hear him say, "I've missed more than 9,000 shots in my career. I've lost almost 300 games. 26 times I've been trusted to take the game winning shot, and missed. I've failed over and over and over again in my life, and that is why I succeed."

My friend who was overwhelmed with fear as he walked among the skyscrapers of Manhattan became one of the best performers in his new company. His family is doing well. Sure, he still battles fear from time to time, because the fear of failure is a part of life. Courage, in this context, involves taking risks despite our fear. And faith in God reassures us that regardless of the outcome of the risks we take, even the worst thing that could happen is not the end of the road. It reminds us that God still rules over the universe even if we fail, and somehow God can bring good even when we fail. Some of the most important successes in my life came on the heels of failures. And that has led me to a great confidence in the words of the Apostle Paul, though they are so frequently quoted they at times seem cliché: "God works all things together for good for the ones who love God, for those who are called according to his purpose" (Romans 8:28).

10

Desperate to Please

At its root, perfectionism isn't really about a deep love of being meticulous. It's about fear. Fear of making a mistake. Fear of disappointing others.

—Michael Law

I like criticism. It makes you strong.

—LeBron James

It's often the case that successful people invite criticism.

—Michael Gove

At the conclusion of each worship service, I stand in the foyer of the church and greet worshippers as they leave. Recently, a woman stopped to say, "I am so profoundly disappointed in your message today—I'm disappointed to call you my pastor." And then she walked away. I wanted to respond, "Well, fine then! Today I'm disappointed to be *your* pastor!" Instead I just stood there, biting my tongue, as she left.

It never feels good to be caught off guard by a cutting remark. When I was younger, it would have eaten at me for a week. But I have come to accept, over nearly thirty years of pastoral ministry, that I *will* disappoint others. Some people will disappoint me. All of us will let others down, and we will experience criticism and rejection as a result.

For those in my church community younger than fifty, fear of disappointing others was the second most frequently cited fear, after fear of failure. For some, the worst words they can hear from others are "I am disappointed in you." Unfortunately, when we allow this fear to control us, it often leads to disastrous consequences. Because criticism and disappointment are sure to come in life, and because at times we need them, learning how to face criticism and disappointment in healthy ways is essential to navigating life successfully.

We were taught as children to say "Sticks and stones may break my bones but words will never harm me" to others who criticized us. But is this true? Of course not. Some of the greatest pain we experience is not physical but emotional, springing from the stinging words of others. This helps explain why our brain tries to keep us away from certain people, activities, or choices. Having known the pain of rejection or criticism in the past, our brain tries to make us steer clear of anything that could hurt us again in the future.

INSTANT, ANONYMOUS, AND NASTY

I suspect that throughout history humans have always been anxious about disappointing others or receiving criticism or experiencing rejection. But we live in a time when people have more opportunities to express disappointment, to offer criticism, and to make public their rejection than ever before. Nearly everyone can offer instant and often anonymous feedback to anyone else at any time. This is terrific for consumers when it comes to reading restaurant reviews on Yelp or deciding what hotel to stay at with the help of TripAdvisor. And Amazon's feedback plays a key role in what books or products I do or don't buy.

But if you run a restaurant, manage a hotel, or sell a book or product on Amazon, you know that these reviews are both a gift and a curse. The gift is that they can help you improve, provided you can read them without getting overly defensive. The challenge is that one in a thousand people may have a bad experience with your product or services and leave you a one-star review while heaping scorn on your business. But wait: If you have only one out of a thousand who is unhappy with your product, those are pretty amazing odds—the equivalent of batting .999 in baseball, an impossible achievement. But let's say your business really is that good. If you serve ten thousand people, however, and you're batting .999, you could see ten negative reviews online, and that would be a lot of one-star reviews.

If you allow your fear of disappointing others and your fear of criticism to control you, you'll struggle to operate any kind of business, to offer any kinds of goods or services, or to provide any kind of leadership at all. Why? Because no matter what you do, you will disappoint someone.

I used to read every review of my books on Amazon, Goodreads, and Barnes & Noble. Inevitably, there would be a review that said, "This is the worst piece of trash I've ever read. I'd give it zero stars if Amazon would let me!" You might have a hundred four- and five-star reviews, but that negative review is the one you'll chew on until you begin to wonder if the reviewer might just be right. In fact, maybe all of your books, not just this one, are trash. My advice: if you are completely undone by disappointing others or receiving negative feedback, don't write books, articles, or blogs.

In our social media age, it is not only business owners, folks in the service industry, and authors who get instant and sometimes uncharitable feedback. Facebook posts, tweets, and every photo we share on Instagram all invite a response or comment and come with the possibility of someone expressing disappointment, indifference, criticism, or rejection. And now a host of emojis make feedback as quick as a click. Of course, some of those cartoon images can be confusing. We understand what a smiley face or a thumbs-up means, but what about this one? 😩 What kind of feedback is that? At least it's safe. Maybe that's why, according to Twitter, the weary face was the most commonly used emoji in America in 2016.

I know more than a few people who finally checked out of social media because of angry, cruel, or insulting comments they received. It was just too painful. Others stopped using social media because they received no comments at all—which they interpreted to mean that no one liked them. Silence felt like its own form of rejection.

280 WAYS TO ZING 'EM

Our conversations on social media become particularly difficult around elections or when we post on political, moral, or religious topics. How do you have a meaningful and helpful conversation about such weighty issues in 280 characters on Twitter? You can't. But 280 characters are perfect for launching zingers, memes, or emojis that do little but rally those who already agree and insult those who don't.

In my own profession, there has always been a tendency to avoid conflict. The Bible describes those who preached only what "itching ears" wanted to hear, without offering a difficult word that was needed or preaching a sermon that might step on the toes of hearers. I could spend my entire ministry steering clear of difficult topics, preaching only sermons that are likely to garner words of affirmation. I expect you face some version of this dynamic in your vocation.

When I teach the art of preaching to pastors, we discuss what is sometimes called prophetic preaching (prophetic not in the sense of telling the future, but in saying difficult things that people may not want to hear). It takes courage to address topics you know might leave people angry, upset, or disappointed. I ask pastors to consider how best to approach the task of saying difficult things. I tell them, "You have to decide: is your goal merely to irritate people, or is it actually to influence them?" It takes little or no skill for a pastor or a public speaker to say things that leave people feeling alienated, wounded, or misrepresented. It takes discernment and considerable skill, on the other hand, to help people hear a difficult word while also positively influencing them to consider it and even act on it. The same is true for all of us, I would suggest, when it comes to difficult conversations on Twitter and Facebook.

QUICK TO LISTEN, SLOW TO SPEAK

Jesus might have had our era in mind when he gave some of his most often cited advice. Take, for example, the Golden Rule: "You should treat people in the same way that you want people to treat you" (Matthew 7:12). He also said that the second greatest commandment is to "love your neighbor as you love yourself" (Matthew 22:39). Further, he told his disciples, "Take the log out of your own eye, and then you'll see clearly to take the speck out of your neighbor's eye" (Matthew 7:5). To those admonitions, we could add the advice of Saint James on how to interact with others: "Be quick to listen, slow to speak, and slow to grow angry" (James 1:19).

These words of scripture should lead a Christian to ask,

"Before I post this comment, share this tweet, offer this meme, or write this review, does it reflect the way I would want to be treated? Am I reflecting love? Am I pointing out the shortcomings of others when I myself have the same or worse shortcomings?"

During the last presidential election season, I asked our congregation to memorize James 1:19 and the Golden Rule from Matthew 7:12. Our church printed the verses on business cards and I asked our people to carry them throughout the campaign, pulling them out for a review before they spoke or posted about politics. I asked them how our conversations and social media posts about politics would be different if we were led by just these two simple verses of scripture. Following the election season, people told me that this small daily reminder changed how they engaged in political conversations.

We experience disappointment, criticism, and rejection when we don't meet other people's expectations. Sometimes they are right to be disappointed. Sometimes we've blown it. In those cases, the criticism or disappointment is an opportunity to grow and to improve—and who doesn't need to do that? Criticism can be a gift if we receive it as such. I've learned that one of the best things I can do is to own my mistakes as quickly as possible, and to humbly and honestly ask for forgiveness.

I've seen, again and again, that a well-timed and sincere apology not only goes a long way toward avoiding losing a member, a customer, or even a friend, but also garners respect from the person to whom it is offered.

Sometimes the disappointment others feel or the criticism they express stems from a misunderstanding. I've found that in those cases, whenever possible, it makes a difference to get together with the other person to listen and talk it through. This happened recently with a longtime member of the church who was upset by something I'd said in a sermon. As we sat down together I asked him to tell me what was bothering him. We had a meaningful conversation, in which I came to understand his concerns. Simply taking the time to listen to him and to acknowledge his views went a long way toward alleviating the disappointment he was feeling. I shared my appreciation for his view, clarified a few misunderstandings, and was able to reaffirm the places where we had differing convictions. In the end, we agreed that we actually were not so far apart, that we could agree to disagree and still love each other. Before parting, we prayed together, embraced, and left with a restored relationship.

But let's be honest: many of us are committed conflict avoiders. Rather than picking up the phone or dropping a note to arrange a meeting like this, we hope the situation just gets better on its own. We do this in part because of our fear of criticism or rejection. Our brain is telling us not to call or to sit down with the other person because it could hurt us to hear their disappointment or criticism. I am a classic conflict avoider. But at my best I force myself to face the conflict by conversing with the individual. Not only does it exponentially increase the chances of reconciliation, it relieves stress for me and the other person.

Sometimes you can't meet with those who are disappointed in you. I can't possibly meet with everyone who ever offered a critical word or a negative tweet, post, response, or review. What helps me overcome the fear of disappointing others, and the criticism and rejection that come with that, is to remember that we all disappoint people at some point. Even the best people I know are criticized and rejected from time to time.

FREEING OURSELVES FROM THE
NEED TO PLEASE

Christians believe that Jesus was not only a good, righteous, compassionate man, but the very incarnation of God. That didn't keep him from being criticized and rejected. "From this time many of his disciples turned back and no longer followed him," we read in John 6:66. In each Gospel, we find the religious authorities insulting him by claiming he was possessed by demons or worked miracles by the power of Satan. Later, at his trial, the crowds chanted, "Crucify him!" Roman soldiers mocked and beat him before nailing him to a cross. And even as he hung from the cross, dying, a crowd stood by hurling insults. Even his closest followers turned away from him in the end.

Our experiences pale in comparison to Jesus's, but his story reminds me that none of us can avoid letting others down, and that suffering from criticism and rejection doesn't necessarily mean we've taken a wrong turn.

Some of us struggle so much with the fear of disappointing others that we might be described as people pleasers, even approval addicts. Professor Sherry Pagoto at the University of Massachusetts Medical School notes that "typically, the intense need to please and care for others is deeply rooted in either a fear of rejection and/or fear of failure. Fear of rejection is the underlying feeling that, *If I don't do everything I can to make this person happy they might leave or stop caring for me.*"

At my more honest moments I think of myself as a recovering people pleaser who occasionally falls off the wagon. As I've aged I've developed a thicker skin and a greater willingness to say and do those things I believe are right, even if it means criticism is sure to follow.

This tendency toward people pleasing is sometimes due to a

lack of secure attachment in childhood that left a child anxious and yearning for more parental love and affirmation than he or she received. In adulthood, the lack of secure human attachment can manifest itself in a persistent fear that others may not love us or think well of us, resulting in regular attempts to win the approval and affection of others by acts of kindness or doing whatever we feel would secure love and affirmation. We all want to be liked, but pleasers have a higher than normal need for others to like them, think well of them, and affirm them. (By the way, many people pleasers are also outstanding conflict avoiders, believing that confronting others is not nice.)

If you recognize your own tendencies in what I've just written, Dr. Harriet Braiker's book *The Disease to Please: Curing the People-Pleasing Syndrome* might prove helpful. I know far too many terrific human beings who wear themselves out trying to be nice, who seem unwilling or unable to ever say no, who feel sure that the affirmation they need will stop coming if they say no. While we all want and need affirmation, it is when our fear of disappointing others, and of rejection by others, controls us that we find ourselves in need of deliverance.

I know parents who are afraid to discipline their children for fear their kids might not like them anymore. If you are a good parent, you will likely face a time when your kids tell you that you are the "meanest parent in the world." But fear of not being your children's friend, or of having them upset with you, is a sure path to bringing pain in the long term to you and your children.

Likewise, if you manage employees, you'll never be the manager your organization needs you to be if you don't say the hard things at times. There are no elected officials who think they can make all of the people happy all of the time—they can't get elected and still believe that.

Among the high costs of people pleasing, I'd point to constant anxiety, accompanied by a lack of boundaries and inadequate self-care. Why do we pay this cost? Because of our fear. All of this activity, all of this work to please others is really about finding love and acceptance for ourselves. What is true in our relationships with others is also true in our relationship with God. I know many people who have desperately tried to win God's approval and love but feel they can never measure up.

HOW GRACE SAVES US

This is where I believe the Christian Gospel, rightly understood, is so powerful. Jesus devoted most of his time to connecting with, teaching, and ministering to "sinners." He ate with them, befriended them, healed them, and taught them about God's mercy and love. He did this before they had done anything that would make them worthy of God's kindness. This is what is meant in the Bible by the word *grace*. Grace is undeserved kindness, blessing, mercy, and love. Grace is grace precisely because we can't earn it.

In his letter to the Ephesians, Saint Paul writes, "God is rich in mercy. He brought us to life with Christ while we were dead as a result of those things that we did wrong. He did this because of the great love that he has for us. You are saved by God's grace!" (2:4–5).

Perhaps you are familiar with the twentieth-century philosopher and theologian Paul Tillich. One of his most famous sermons was titled "You Are Accepted." The message reaches its climax in this powerful and oft-quoted section:

Grace . . . strikes us when our disgust for our own being, our indifference, our weakness, our hostility, and our lack

of direction and composure have become intolerable to us.
It strikes us when, year after year, the longed-for perfec-
tion of life does not appear, when the old compulsions
reign within us as they have for decades, when despair
destroys all joy and courage.

Sometimes at that moment a wave of light breaks into
our darkness, and it is as though a voice were saying:
"You are accepted. You are accepted, accepted by that
which is greater than you, and the name of which you
do not know. Do not ask for the name now; perhaps you
will find it later. Do not try to do anything now; perhaps
later you will do much. Do not seek for anything; do not
perform anything; do not intend anything. Simply accept
the fact that you are accepted!" If that happens to us, we
experience grace.

Yes! When we finally trust in this grace, this acceptance and
love of God, we can stop trying to manipulate others into giving love and acceptance to us by our niceness. We can truly live,
and truly love—not pretending to love so that we might receive
love, but serving out of an abundance of love, freely giving love
without expecting anything in return.

I'd like to close this chapter by returning to the importance
of finding the courage to overcome a closely related fear—our
fear of criticism.

Giving in to the fear of criticism practically guarantees that
you'll miss out on life, and miss out on faithfully doing what
God wants you to do. Jesus noted, "Happy are you when people insult you and harass you and speak all kinds of bad and
false things about you, all because of me. Be full of joy and be
glad, because you have a great reward in heaven" (Matthew

5:11–12*a*). Most of the great leaders in scripture were criticized when they began doing what God called them to do.

The greatest leaders, and the people who have a significant impact on the world, are not those who were never criticized. Instead, they are those who, when criticized, did not give up.

HE REFUSED TO GIVE UP

I think about Doane Robinson. He was a lawyer turned state historian who died in 1946. Robinson had a bold idea for getting people to travel to his home state, South Dakota, one very few people ever visited. He wanted to create a massive sculpture out of the side of a mountain. Environmentalists, Native Americans, and many South Dakotans lambasted the idea, severely criticizing the state historian and expressing their disappointment in his idea and in him. He wanted to be liked, yet he refused to give up in the face of criticism and rejection. Because he persisted, today Mount Rushmore is one of the most iconic sculptures in the United States and every year over two million people travel to South Dakota just to see it.

Courage, as we've seen, is not the elimination of fear. Courage is doing what we know we should do in the face of rejection—choosing not to give up in the face of criticism. And grace is the truth that when others are disappointed, even when you've truly blown it, there is One whose love and acceptance remains steadfast.

11

Meaningless

Life is never made unbearable by circumstances, but only by lack of meaning and purpose.

—Viktor Frankl

He who has a why to live for can bear almost any how.

—Friedrich Nietzsche

N THE THREE MONTHS BEFORE I SAT DOWN TO WRITE THIS chapter, ten people took their own lives in my community. Some were church members. Most were friends or family of church members. Several were young adults. All were persons who had struggled with depression, or who lost, at least for a moment, a sense that life mattered, who lost hope and a reason to go on.

The psychotherapist Viktor Frankl, who survived Hitler's death camps, devoted much of his life to understanding what makes human beings tick, including the circumstances that cause them to either give up or retain hope. Prior to the Holocaust, while he was still in medical school, Frankl began a free and successful program to help teens struggling with suicidal thoughts. Building on its success, he later began a similar program at Vienna's General Hospital, where he and others treated tens of thousands of women who contemplated ending their lives. In 1942, he and his wife, Tilly, were sent to a concentration camp. Viktor survived, but Tilly and much of the rest of his family died in the camps.

It was Frankl's reflections on his experiences in the death camps and what he observed of his fellow prisoners that led him to write the remarkable book *Man's Search for Meaning* (first titled *Saying Yes to Life in Spite of Everything*). Written soon after the war, and revised several times since, the book opens with Frankl's fascinating firsthand account of being arrested and sent to the camps and of daily life in them. In the second half of the book, he describes his approach to psychotherapy, which in large part was shaped by his experiences in the camps.

Central to Frankl's approach to psychotherapy, and to our purpose in this chapter, was his observation that a prisoner who lost a sense of meaning or purpose in his or her life soon gave in to the horrors of the camps and was likely to die. But prisoners who found meaning in their suffering, or felt there was some significance to life, were likely to summon the strength to carry on.

When Frankl spoke of finding meaning in his own suffering, he was not saying that "everything happens for a reason"—that God somehow intended things like Hitler's gas chambers and concentration camps. The God whose very nature is love does not will the slaughter of millions of people.* Much of what happens in the world is clearly *not* God's will—injustice, hate, bigotry, violence, poverty, rape, cruelty, self-centeredness, abuse . . . the list goes on. When things that are not God's will do happen, Frankl taught, there is an opportunity for us to find

---

* See my book *Why? Making Sense of God's Will* (Nashville, TN: Abingdon Press, 2011).

and create meaning from them. In *Man's Search for Meaning* he offered as examples the prisoners in his camp who acted with love, compassion, or mercy despite the inhumane conditions they endured. These prisoners had a strength and resilience in facing their circumstances.

As Frankl noted in the preface to the book's 1992 edition, "Life holds a potential meaning under any conditions, even the most miserable ones."* This became the basis of his school of psychotherapy, which Frankl called logotherapy. The Greek word *logos* is often translated as "word," but *logos* also conveys the idea of "meaning." For Frankl, "this striving to find a meaning in one's life is the primary motivational force in man."**

MEANT TO MAKE A DIFFERENCE

Many of us are never consciously aware that the search for meaning is a fundamental human need. What we may notice, though, is an unsettled feeling—a struggle with a vague, or sometimes intense, sense that something is not right or that life feels flat or unsatisfying. Rather than use this observation as an occasion to search for meaning, our thoughts often give way to fear that life simply has no meaning. Understandably, this fear may lead to despair.

I believe our deep need for a meaningful life was placed within our hearts by our Creator. Scripture speaks of God creating humankind in God's image, or what theologians call the *imago Dei*. Part of the image of God seen in us is found in our

---

* Viktor E. Frankl, *Man's Search for Meaning* (Boston: Beacon Press, 1992), Kindle edition, preface.

** Ibid., Kindle edition, Part II.

yearning for a purpose greater than ourselves. While Frankl's logotherapy doesn't require one to have faith, I connect with it because the Christian faith assumes that we have purpose—that there is a meaning to our lives.

I asked two thirty-year-olds recently about their greatest fears. One immediately replied, "I fear a life of insignificance; that I won't have made a difference at all." The other said something similar: "I fear not living up to my potential—not having done as much as I could have done and should have done to impact others and the world." Interestingly, beneath the fears of both of these young adults is an underlying belief that human beings are meant to make a difference, to somehow positively affect others and the world around us.

These young people are typical of many millennials. Unlike their parents, who were often more motivated by money or success or acquisition at their age, today's twenty- and thirty-somethings have made meaningful experiences, significant relationships, and purposeful work much higher priorities. In fact, I've met some young people who were so focused on these higher goals that they struggled with how to integrate them with the "real world," where most people have to work at more mundane jobs. What they may not have learned yet is that most people work ordinary jobs while finding and creating meaning in and through them. I think of the insurance salesman who told me that he loved his job as it gave him the opportunity to focus on helping his clients and prospects. Or the sacker at the supermarket who sought to bless each of his store's customers with words of kindness. Or the construction worker who told me he envisioned that the work he did was, as the New Testament teaches, for the Lord and not just for his client.

In his bestselling book *The Purpose Driven Life*, Rick Warren struck a nerve with baby boomers and gen Xers who were beginning to doubt that wealth and success could satisfy something deep in their hearts. This was particularly true for middle- and upper-middle-income people who were not struggling to make ends meet. The book helped millions of people think more clearly about ultimate concerns. I remember one parishioner who struggled with anxiety and found that focusing on the purpose of her life played a significant role in easing the anxiety and panic she was wrestling with.

THE UPSIDE-DOWN WAY OF JESUS

Jesus challenged the self-absorbed, materialistic approach to life, sometimes with simple questions like this one: "What good is it for someone to gain the whole world, and yet lose or forfeit their very self?" (Luke 9:25). He also noted, in that same context, "All who want to save their lives will lose them" (Luke 9:24). In this passage Jesus offers a paradox. He says that it is in self-denial and laying down our lives that we find life. Or as Saint Francis of Assisi famously noted, "It is in giving that we receive."

Americans have placed a lot of stock in the "pursuit of happiness." But Jesus's words tell us that happiness is the result of something else—of self-denial, laying down our lives, and following him. All of which parallels what Frankl noted in his preface to the 1992 edition of *Man's Search for Meaning*:

> For success, like happiness, cannot be pursued; it must ensue, and it only does so as the unintended side-effect of one's dedication to a cause greater than oneself or as the by-product of one's surrender to a person other than oneself. Happiness must happen, and the same holds for success: you have to let it happen by not caring about it. I

want you to listen to what your conscience commands you
to do and go on to carry it out to the best of your knowl-
edge. Then you will live to see that in the long run—in the
long run, I say!—success will follow you precisely because
you had forgotten to think of it.

Frankl's mention of listening to our conscience and doing what it commands points to where we find those causes greater than ourselves. His answer is our conscience—that voice we hear within calling us to be our best self by serving others and doing what we know is right. But I know people whose consciences seem faulty, who never really feel the nudge or whisper to rise above a narcissistic, self-absorbed life. That's because our consciences are shaped by other forces—our parents, our society, our spiritual communities and practices.

So what is that cause or purpose greater than ourselves to which we are meant to surrender, the by-product of which will be happiness? My personal answer to that question comes from my faith and what it teaches about God's purpose for human existence.

CREATED TO GIVE AND RECEIVE LOVE

The creation stories at the beginning of the Bible point to the idea that God created humankind to be recipients of God's love, to reciprocate God's love, and to take care of the world that God has made. We see these ideas consistently throughout the scriptures. Nearly every Christian can recite Jesus's response to the question "What is the most important commandment?" Jesus responded with not one commandment but two: "You must love the Lord your God with all your heart, with all your being, and with all your mind. This is the first and greatest commandment. And the second is like it: You must love your neighbor as you love yourself. All the Law and the Prophets depend on these two commands" (Matthew 22:37–40).

According to Jesus, our daily lives are meant to be lived in the rhythm of accepting and reciprocating God's love, loving our neighbors, and pursuing God's will in tangible ways. Loving our neighbors does not mean having warm, fuzzy feelings for them. It means, in the words of an eighth-century-BC Hebrew prophet, "to do justice, and to love kindness, and to walk humbly with your God" (Micah 6:8*b*). To do justice and to practice loving-kindness is to bless, encourage, serve, and seek the best for those around us. Grand as that may sound, this mission is something that can be pursued in our day-in, day-out living, beginning with simple acts. I wake up each morning, slip to my knees next to my bed, and pray, "Thank you, God, for today. Thank you for your love and grace. I offer myself once more to you today. Please help me to be mindful of those around me. Use me to bless, encourage, and show kindness to all that I meet today. Send me on your mission today." Every moment and every encounter throughout the day is an opportunity for you to live a meaningful, purposeful, missional existence.

We can fear that our lives will have been insignificant or meaningless unless we accomplish something big. But that is a false fear. Clearly, few people accomplish something truly "big" with their lives—and it is not the "big" thing that will ensure that our lives have meaning. Rather, the sum total of hundreds and thousands of small acts that we do across the course of our lives is what truly gives our lives meaning. "Small things done with great love will change the world" is commonly cited as Saint Teresa of Calcutta's words to live by

What do those small things done with great love actually look like? They include speaking words of kindness, affirmation, and encouragement—or better, delivering a handwritten note expressing the same. Small things include being a wise steward of our energy resources: for example, turning the lights off when you leave a room. They look like buying someone else's lunch, anonymously, in order to bless them, or stopping to see your sick neighbor in the hospital, or providing comfort and hope to a coworker who has just lost a loved one. They look like volunteering to serve others in need. Most of these things require a bit of thoughtfulness and a willingness to get nothing in return. But you do get something in return. You reduce that nagging sense that your life might not matter today. And you receive joy.

Meaningful and significant lives are lived moment by moment—as we pay attention to the world around us, as we give thanks to God from whom all of life is a gift, as we look for the simple and selfless ways that we can love and serve others while positively impacting our world. It is both an attitude of the heart and a rhythm of daily actions that affect us as much as we affect others.

"WHAT IF . . . ?": THE SECRET POWER OF SMALL THINGS

I met with a young man whom I'll call Alex. Alex regularly struggled with feelings of insignificance. In fact, he felt certain that he was trapped in a meaningless existence. When I asked Alex to describe his picture of a meaningful life, he spoke of accomplishing some great thing. He'd spent several years trying to find that "great thing," but to no avail. I commended him for his desire to do something meaningful, but after we had talked for a while, I challenged him to think differently about the kind of actions that constitute a meaningful life. "What if,"

I proposed to Alex, "meaning and significance are not usually found in big accomplishments but in a couple of dozen small things you do every week?"

Then I told him about Maybelle. In her little dog mind, I've noticed that her greatest joy (if one can attribute such a thing to a dog) seems to be found in letting my wife and me love her, and in loving us in return. Maybelle loves to jump into the bed first thing in the morning and start licking my face to wake me up (which leaves me giggling, even at fifty-three). In the evening when I get home from work, she is there wagging her tail, turning circles, and jumping up and down, hoping for me to stop and show her love. Taking a lesson from Maybelle's devotion, I turned the conversation with Alex to how God's love can reframe our search for meaning. "Our greatest purpose in life is to be loved by God, and to love God, and to reflect God's love in tangible ways to others," I said. "I believe that as you and I do that, we will find ourselves living the life God intends for us."

Alex is still hoping to find his "big" thing, but he's begun taking seriously the idea that every day presents each of us with dozens of opportunities to pursue justice and to practice loving-kindness. He's begun seizing those opportunities, and as he does, he is finding meaning for his life.

I'm not suggesting that we are merely God's pets, as Maybelle is to LaVon and me, but instead that just as Maybelle takes joy and satisfaction in the companionship of her master and doing his will, we too might see our purpose, joy, and satisfaction as somehow connected to God's companionship and doing God's will. The Westminster Catechism, drafted in the seventeenth century, is best known for the question "What is the chief end of man?" and the response "To glorify God and to enjoy him forever." To glorify God includes giving praise and thanks to God, but it also includes living a life that is pleasing to God. It includes seeking to do justice and practicing kindness. It includes looking for ways to love our neighbors and take care of God's creation. It includes offering yourself to God to do God's will. This is, for Christians, the cause that is greater than ourselves.

MADE FOR JOY RIGHT NOW

And don't miss the second part of the Catechism's statement of our purpose. We're also meant to enjoy God, and I think this includes our trust in God's love, our loving God in return, and our enjoying the world that God has made. For much of my life, my workaholic tendencies left little room for pleasure and enjoyment. Today I realize that the God who gave us the Sabbath to rest, who created the amazing world that we live in, wishes us to enjoy our lives, just as I wish for my children to enjoy theirs. Saint Paul captures this when he writes that God "richly provides everything for our enjoyment" (1 Timothy 6:17c).

You don't have to fear living a meaningless or insignificant life. And it is not terribly hard to find a life full of meaning. For me, meaning is found in my faith, in gratefully receiving the good things in life as gifts from God, in seeking to walk with my Master and to do his will, and in seeing each day, and every encounter, as an opportunity to fulfill God's purposes for my life.

There is a certain rhythm to the Catechism's statement about the "chief end" to which we are intended to devote ourselves. It is a kind of sacred dance, this rhythm of giving and receiving. We seek to live moment by moment as God would have us live, doing God's work, pursuing love and justice, mercy and kindness, and giving thanks to God, *and* we seek to gratefully and joyfully experience and savor the blessings inherent in the world God has given us. We fear meaninglessness. But in this wonderful tension of both giving and receiving, we find our lives become meaning-full.

12

Alone and Unloved

We're all a bit scared of loneliness—of being alone.
Of being left. Of not being loved. Or needed.
Or cared about. "Lonely" hits a spot of fear in all of us
even if we don't acknowledge it.*

—SUE BOURNE, producer of the BBC documentary
The Age of Loneliness

WE ALL FEEL LONELY AT TIMES. I HAVE A FAMILY MEM-
ber who calls herself a hermit—she doesn't really feel
the need for much in the way of companionship. But I sense
that there are moments when she feels lonely. I know a guy
who jokes about not wanting or needing friends. Yet I don't
know where he would be without his dog. I have hundreds, if
not a thousand, phone numbers on my contact lists, and tens
of thousands of "friends" on Facebook. Yet there are moments
when I feel alone.

Loneliness is the feeling of sadness that comes from a sense
of social isolation—from feeling alone as though we have no
real companions with whom to share our life.

Loneliness is not the same as solitude. We all need solitude

---

* Sue Bourne, "10 Reasons People Are Lonely? It's More Complicated
Than That," *The Guardian*, January 4, 2016.

from time to time. Not long ago, I went through a stretch without any evening meetings—unusual for me. By the third evening, just as I was settling into the living room, attempting to strike up a conversation with LaVon as she was trying to read, she said to me, "Isn't there some ministry that needs you tonight, or someone you need to visit in the hospital?" We both laughed, but her comment revealed something I'd missed. I was intruding on my wife's alone time.

We do need times of solitude, but we are also wired as human beings for companionship—for people we can share our lives with, talk to, listen to—people who care about us and enjoy being with us. That mysterious dance of two powerful but opposite needs will be the focus of our conversation in this chapter. Whether you enjoy a rich web of relationships today, or find yourself standing alone in your kitchen too many nights, wishing with all your heart that someone you love was coming home for dinner, we all will struggle with the fear of being alone at times. The focus of this chapter is particularly timely if you are currently suffering the pain of loneliness.

GOD'S FIRST *"NOT* GOOD"

The seventeenth-century poet John Milton wrote "loneliness is the first thing which God's eye named not good." Milton was referencing Genesis 2, in which God places the first human in the Garden of Eden and then says, "It is not good that the human is alone." At the very beginning of scripture we find the human need for companionship.

Not everyone is meant to be married, but everyone, even the most introverted of us, needs some human connection. We begin the first nine months of our lives nestled within another human being. We are knit together, becoming human, hearing our mother's heartbeat and the sound of her voice, her breathing, her muffled words. During that time we're never alone. Is it any wonder that when we're tiny infants we wake up in the middle of the night crying, often not for food or to be changed, but simply to be held. The fear of being alone begins at our birth.

The British psychologist John Bowlby (1907–90) pioneered the field of attachment theory. He had a major impact on the disciplines of parenting, child psychology, and relationship therapy. He believed that we are genetically predisposed to have a few significant relationships in our lives. He showed that our earliest childhood experiences with our primary caregiver can have a significant impact on our ability to have healthy relationships with others. If our earliest relationship experiences are healthy and secure, we're more likely to be able to enjoy secure relationships later on. But if we experience emotional abandonment, neglect, abuse, or erratic and unpredictable care in childhood, or the loss of a parent or caregiver, our ability to enter into secure and healthy relationships with others may be jeopardized.

Bowlby's research explains why each of us approaches relationships differently, depending on where we fall on the attachment spectrum. He identified three styles of attachment: secure, anxious, and avoidant. Individuals with a *secure attachment* style find it easy to be in strong, healthy, and loving relationships. They likely experienced a healthy attachment with a caregiver when they were very young. Individuals with an *anxious attachment* style, in contrast, fear that their mates or friends or others close to them do not love them as much as the anxiously attached person loves his or her friends. They tend to be hypersensitive, get their feelings hurt too easily, misread the feelings and responses of others to them, and are quick to feel rejected or unloved.

The third style of attachment is *avoidant attachment*. These individuals, having been wounded by the lack of adequate love or nurturing when they were children, learned to cope by becoming emotionally self-sufficient and independent, not needing, and perhaps even struggling to accept, love and intimacy. Attempts by others to be close to them may leave them feeling emotionally suffocated. Interestingly, sometimes anxious attachers find themselves drawn to avoiders, which creates an unhealthy cycle in which the anxious attacher seeks love and affirmation, the avoider feels smothered, and the anxious attacher becomes even more anxious and desperate for affirmation, pushing the avoider even further away.*

"I WILL LEAVE YOU FIRST"

A woman in my congregation who identifies as an anxious attacher described her personal battle with the fear of loneliness:

> *Rejection for me came at an early age. Loneliness soon followed, then mental illness and relational conflicts. I have been in beautiful relationships that I have destroyed because I was afraid of others leaving me. My mantra was "I will leave you before you have a chance to leave me."* . . . *Everything that they do is scrutinized or tested to see if they still care for me. And when I finally test them beyond*

---

* Some psychologists use slightly different categories for those with insecure attachment, including anxious-preoccupied, dismissive-avoidant, and fearful-avoidant.

what they can bear, it breaks both hearts. . . . Those I care for the most are the ones that I fear losing the most. It is hell on earth that I experience daily.

Estimates vary, but research done in the late 1980s surveying 1,200 individuals found that 56 percent of the population are in the secure range of attachment, 25 percent are in the avoidant range, and 19 percent are in the anxious range (these traits are on a spectrum and can change over time, with most of us exhibiting some secure, anxious, and avoidant tendencies).[*] If you are interested in learning more about your attachment traits, there are online surveys you can take.[**] Those in romantic relationships or seeking romantic relationships can choose from a host of books written on attachment.[***] If attachment sounds like something you wrestle with, I encourage you to find a therapist who specializes in attachment theory. A trained specialist can help you identify the root causes of your attachment issue, the tendencies related to it, and strategies for adapting and moving toward secure and healthy attachment.

Not all loneliness springs from attachment concerns. It may be that we've recently experienced the loss of a friend, or we struggle in knowing how to develop meaningful relationships, or we're going through a period of isolation or depression. For some, the experience of loneliness in the present can lead to

---

[*] Cindy Hazan and Phillip Shaver, "Romantic Love Conceptualized as an Attachment Process," *Journal of Personality and Social Psychology* 52, no. 3 (March 1987): 511–24.

[**] This survey took about ten minutes and offered some helpful insights: http://www.yourpersonality.net/attachment/index.php.

[***] Many people have been helped by Amir Levine and Rachel Heller's book *Attached: The New Science of Adult Attachment and How It Can Help You Find—and Keep—Love* (New York: Penguin, 2010).

a fear of being alone and unloved in the future. Once more we catastrophize: we tell ourselves things like "I'm not smart enough," "I'm too fat," "No one likes me, and no one *will ever* like me," or simply "I am lonely now and I'll always feel lonely and there is nothing I can do about it. I'm going to be alone forever, and I'll grow old and die alone."

One of the members of the church I pastor wrote to tell me that at age sixty-two his wife had died. They'd been married for forty-two years—since they were twenty. He said, "It hit me hard that I was all alone in this empty house. Fear set in—now what? Was I going to have to endure this empty feeling the rest of my life?" This fear of loneliness in the future is particularly pronounced when we lose a spouse.

It is easy for any of us to think that if we were just more famous, talented, attractive, wealthy, or we had a wider social circle, we'd be spared this affliction. Yet there's plenty of evidence that loneliness afflicts the rich and the poor, the very well known and the obscure. Albert Einstein once wrote, "It is a strange thing to be so widely known, and yet to be so lonely." When she was twenty-two, the Oscar-winning actress Anne Hathaway noted, "Loneliness is my least favorite thing about life. The thing that I'm most worried about is just being alone without anybody to care for or someone who will care for me."

Loneliness, like fear, is a part of life. It usually passes. But chronic loneliness can have serious emotional and physical consequences. One study in Great Britain said that sustained periods of loneliness can have the same impact on your physical health as smoking fifteen cigarettes a day.

In countries like Great Britain and America, researchers are now speaking of an "epidemic of loneliness." According to the latest Census Bureau data, Americans move, on average, slightly more than eleven times during their lifetimes, and each time they do so they lose meaningful relationships.* People used to have only two or three jobs in a lifetime, and many of their most significant relationships developed in the workplace. But now, an article in *Fast Company* noted, those who want to get ahead in the workplace "should plan on switching jobs every three years for . . . life."** What does that do for developing significant long-term relationships?

When we retire, we say good-bye to our work relationships. People who relocate to sunny places like Florida or Arizona leave behind neighbors and friends and their church family. All of a sudden, they're tasked with rebuilding a network of new friends at sixty-five or seventy. Sometimes relocating works out great, but sometimes it undercuts long-term relationships developed over a lifetime. Divorce too leads to loneliness because one of the casualties of divorce is often a couple's entire network of friends.

LOSING THE EXPERIENCE OF TOUCH

Technology can help us stay connected, but it often leaves us more isolated than in the past. We speak in 280-character tweets and short text messages but often at the expense of hearing each other's voices, looking into each other's eyes, or experiencing the touch of another person. When things are going rough, we send our friends a sad face emoji or a text message expressing sympathy and consolation, but an emoji can't take the place of a hug.

---

* Adam Chandler, "Why Do Americans Move So Much More Than Europeans?," *The Atlantic,* October 21, 2016.

** Vivian Giang, "You Should Plan on Switching Jobs Every Three Years for the Rest of Your Life," *Fast Company,* January 7, 2016.

In an article in *The Atlantic* titled "Have Smartphones Destroyed a Generation?," Jean Twenge, a professor of psychology at San Diego State University, describes young people born between 1995 and 2012 as the iGen, referring to the fact that most of them, even those raised in lower-income families, will have a smartphone as they grow up. Twenge notes, "It's not an exaggeration to describe iGen as being on the brink of the worst mental-health crisis in decades. Much of this deterioration can be traced to their phones. . . . The number of teens who get together with their friends nearly every day dropped by more than 40 percent from 2000 to 2015."[*] It might appear from Twenge's research that the loneliness epidemic is just getting started.

In light of all of these factors that play a role in developing and maintaining meaningful relationships, how can we overcome loneliness, and live without fear of future loneliness and of being unloved?

People who fear loneliness tend to interpret social interactions in the most negative way possible. If someone doesn't respond to my e-mail within an hour or a day, it can't be because they were busy or missed the e-mail; it must mean they don't like me. If someone walks by without talking to or looking at me, it can't be because they are preoccupied; it must mean they are mad at me. If someone is in a bad mood, it can't be because they have other problems; it must mean they don't want to be around me. I know so many people who have these thoughts; occasionally, I've had them myself.

As with other fears, part of what we've learned is to exam-

---

[*] Jean M. Twenge, "Have Smartphones Destroyed a Generation?," *The Atlantic*, September 2017.

ine our assumptions in light of the facts. We've also learned to recognize our catastrophizing tendencies, to choose not to jump to conclusions, and to assume the best instead of the worst of the other.*

When I was in college, I sold women's shoes in a department store. One day, a couple came into the store looking at shoes, picking up various samples from the display cases. I stood behind them and said, "Hi! Can I help you find something today?" But neither responded. I waited for a few moments and asked again. Still no response. I waited a few minutes more and asked again. Still no response! I found myself getting irritated. Did they think so poorly of a shoe salesman that they didn't even feel they needed to reply? We sold expensive women's shoes, so I figured they were wealthy people who thought they were too good to speak to me, a lowly clerk, until they wanted something.

As I stood there stewing, the couple turned around. Only then did I notice that they were communicating to each other in sign language. I had jumped to the conclusion that they were intentionally ignoring me, but obviously they hadn't heard a word I'd said. I realized that I was the rude one, having not shown enough respect to approach them face-to-face.

LEARNING TO REENGAGE

Often when we feel lonely or fear being alone, we tend to do the opposite of what is needed. Instead of reaching out to others, or going out where others are, we withdraw in fear. We drop

---

* Heidi Grant Halvorson, Ph.D., "The Cure for Loneliness," *Psychology Today,* October 1, 2010.

out. We stop trying to connect. It feels easier and less painful to isolate ourselves. And it almost guarantees that our struggles will continue.

One of the commonsense responses that address this kind of fear is simply to reengage with others, no matter what that might feel like at first. I've watched as isolators who'd retired took on part-time jobs that gave them social interaction with others. I've seen many introverted singles volunteer at the church and develop meaningful relationships there. For some, the strategy for combating loneliness may include getting a pet—someone to talk to—though pets cannot fully serve as surrogates for people. The older we get, the more important reengagement becomes. If your struggle is intense, and you find yourself regularly wrestling with loneliness, you might want to talk to a pastor or a therapist in your community who can help you evaluate what's not working in your attempts to develop friendships and to develop a personalized plan for how to change this.

As we mature, most Americans spend a great deal of time focused on financial security in retirement. But researchers note that the single most important indicator of your happiness in retirement is not how much money you have in your 401(k) but the quality of your relationships. If you invest as much in your long-term relationships as you do in your 401(k), you're likely to live a longer, healthier, and happier life.

Recognizing the health costs of loneliness, Great Britain started the Campaign to End Loneliness; its first goal is to ensure that "people most at risk of loneliness are reached and supported."[*] One community started a phone line that lonely

---

[*] Campaign to End Lonelieness: Connections in Older Age, https://www.campaigntoendloneliness.org/.

people could call just to talk to someone who would listen. Named the Silver Line, it received 428,000 calls in 2016. At Resurrection, we developed a ministry years ago called Silver Link. On a weekly basis, our members visit thirty-five area nursing homes and senior care centers to develop friendships and to care for senior adults, many of whom have no grandchildren or children in town who visit them. We also sponsor an adopt-a-pet program through which our members take their pets to visit seniors and offer a host of other services aimed at helping the elderly find meaningful connections.

Volunteers who visit the nursing homes and care centers find that their own loneliness is pushed aside as they seek to help seniors who are isolated and alone. That is what Saint Francis of Assisi gave expression to eight hundred years ago when he wrote, "It is in giving that we receive," and what Jesus meant when he said, "It is more blessed to give than to receive."

And that leads me to one last, but I think ultimately very important, strategy for addressing our fear of being alone and unloved: getting involved in a vibrant local church. I first discovered this as a fourteen-year-old high school freshman. I didn't believe in God at the time, but I got involved in a youth group where I developed some of the deepest friendships of my life. My wife and I experienced this as newlyweds in a new city where we knew no one, but came to develop meaningful relationships with the people in a Sunday school class. I think about the night in seminary, five hundred miles away from our family, when LaVon went into labor with our first daughter, and two couples from our church stayed from 6 p.m. until midnight in the waiting room just so we'd know someone was there.

An AARP study that came out a couple of years ago noted that people involved in their church, synagogue, or mosque were 40 percent less likely to report a sense of loneliness than those who were not. Study after study has found that people who have faith and are actively involved in a faith community are not only happier and less lonely but also healthier and live longer. Many young adults today are longing for authentic community. The church is intended to be exactly that.

But even in a church, developing relationships requires effort and intentionality.

When LaVon and I started the Church of the Resurrection, we had two small children, and taking care of them and a growing church left little time for friends. We went five years without being involved in any kind of small group. By that time, more than two thousand people were attending worship each weekend. One day I looked at LaVon and said, "We have thousands of people in this church, and I am their pastor, but I feel lonely. We have got to do something to get to know people and develop friendships." LaVon is a bit of an introvert, but she agreed. We invited six couples—some of whom we knew well, some of whom we didn't know too well—to meet with us weekly for Bible study or to read and discuss books like the one you are reading now. I can honestly say that this decision significantly changed our lives for the better, and over the years we developed lifelong friendships. We've raised our kids together. We've gone on mission trips together. We've visited one another in the hospital. We've laughed and cried with one another. And we'll grow old together in the years ahead. But that didn't just happen; we had to be intentional in developing these relationships. It takes some people multiple attempts before they find a group, a Sunday school class, or a church where they are finally able to develop these connections. If that's been your experience, don't give up. If you've done this in the past but dropped out, maybe it's time to try it again.

THE AMAZING FAITH OF FRIENDS

In the Gospels we read about a paralyzed man who was carried on a stretcher by four friends in the hope that Jesus might pray for him. Interestingly, neither account of the story (Matthew 9, Mark 2) mentions that the paralyzed man asked for help. But clearly his friends cared enough to make sure he got in front of the healer from Nazareth. Because of *their* faith, Jesus said—not the man's faith, but that of his friends—the man was healed. We all need friends like that. At Resurrection, we call them "stretcher bearers." Stretcher bearers are the handful of people who love you so much they will be there for you, carry you when you can't walk, and stand with you through thick and thin. But in some ways, though it sounds trite or cliché, the only way to have a friend (or stretcher bearer) is to be one.

This is what church is supposed to look like: not just people worshipping together, but people in relationships who are volunteering together, growing together, studying together, and playing together—doing life together in a vibrant web of community. In a very real sense, the entire New Testament can be read as an instruction manual for how to live together in Christian community.

I agree with those existentialist philosophers who have described loneliness as a fundamental part of the human condition. But I don't think they should stop there. You and I are meant for relationships with others. As a Christian, I believe that our loneliness is not only a yearning for friendship with others but also a yearning for God's love and a daily, deep relationship with him. Perhaps you've heard Saint Augustine's prayer and affirmation of faith: "Thou hast made us for thyself, O Lord, and our heart is restless until it finds its rest in thee."

The deep longing in our hearts is in part a longing for companionship with God.

This idea of friendship or companionship with God is not some esoteric state achieved only by the great mystics. On multiple occasions in scripture ordinary people are described as "friends" of God. Abraham is called the friend of God in scripture,* and Exodus 33:11 says that God spoke to Moses as a man speaks to a friend. The Psalms reflect the deep relationship God's people might have with God. And, just before his own death, Jesus said to his disciples, "I do not call you servants any longer, because the servant does not know what the master is doing; but I have called you friends" (John 15:15).

Joseph Scriven famously captured the promise of friendship with God through Jesus in a poem he wrote in 1855, which later became the well-loved gospel hymn "What a Friend We Have in Jesus." I love the third verse, in particular:

> *Are we weak and heavy-laden,*
> *Cumbered with a load of care?*
> *Precious Savior, still our refuge—*
> *Take it to the Lord in prayer;*
> *Do thy friends despise, forsake thee?*
> *Take it to the Lord in prayer;*
> *In His arms He'll take and shield thee,*
> *Thou wilt find a solace there.*

AS NEAR AS THE AIR YOU BREATHE

One important dimension of the Christian spiritual life is what some people call their "personal relationship with Jesus Christ."

---

* 2 Chronicles 20:7 and James 2:23

The phrase is a turnoff for others—it feels somehow sappy and trite. But for me this dimension of Christian spirituality is the most life-giving of all.

Rather than believing that I'm unloved, and will never be loved, I trust that I am *already* loved with a love that will never let me go, a love that was demonstrated in Christ's life, teachings, death, and resurrection. I trust that God is with me, as near as the air that I breathe. Consequently, I speak to him, listen for him, and at times pour out my heart to him. He is, for me, the embodiment of presence, love, and mercy. I love how the psalmist captures the nearness of God to us in Psalm 139:5, 7–10:

> *You hem me in, behind and before,*
> *and lay your hand upon me. . . .*
> *Where can I go from your spirit?*
> *Or where can I flee from your presence?*
> *If I ascend to heaven, you are there;*
> *if I make my bed in Sheol, you are there.*
> *If I take the wings of the morning*
> *and settle at the farthest limits of the sea,*
> *even there your hand shall lead me,*
> *and your right hand shall hold me fast.*

You can harness the power of your imagination to conjure up a future in which you are alone and unloved. Or you can use that same power to imagine the truth of the scriptures that say that there is a God who knows you, who loves you, and who is always by your side. You are loved with a love that will not let you go. Imagine that!

Part Four

APOCALYPSE, CHANGE, MISSING OUT, AND FINANCES

13

A Dystopian Future

Opposite of utopia [handwritten annotation]

We face awesome environmental challenges: climate change, food production, overpopulation, the decimation of other species, epidemic disease, acidification of the oceans. . . . We are at the most dangerous moment in the development of humanity.[*]

—STEPHEN HAWKING

Then I saw a new heaven and a new earth, for the former heaven and the former earth had passed away.

—REVELATION 21:1

*D*YSTOPIA. THE WORD CAPTURES OUR WORST FEARS about a bleak future. It describes the opposite of utopia, the ideal future. Two of the classics most of us read in school were George Orwell's *1984* and Aldous Huxley's *Brave New World*. Both paint a picture of a future where totalitarianism has created something of a living hell. More recently, Cormac McCarthy's Pulitzer Prize–winning novel *The Road* took readers to a future where much of America has been destroyed by an unidentified planetary holocaust. Dystopian film series like

---

[*] Stephen Hawking, "This Is the Most Dangerous Time for Our Planet," *The Guardian*, December 1, 2016.

Planet of the Apes, Mad Max, and *The Hunger Games* offer similarly bleak views of the future.

The reason these apocalyptic and dystopian visions are the stuff of summer blockbusters and bestselling novels is because they tap into our deep-seated fears about the future. Most of us are just a bit afraid that the world really is coming to a terrifying end. I've seen this fear about the future over the years in the congregation I serve, among people I know and care about. Our scientists, politicians, and preachers at times feed this fear of grim times ahead.

Stephen Hawking's quote at the top of the chapter provides his recent assessment of the impending environmental dangers. The journalist Ted Koppel wrote a book a couple of years ago called *Lights Out: A Cyberattack, a Nation Unprepared, Surviving the Aftermath,* which, as the title makes clear, points to the threat of attacks on our power grid. More recently, the billionaire tech entrepreneur Elon Musk (Tesla, SpaceX, PayPal) has been warning about the danger of AI, artificial intelligence, and how, in the future, this technology could lead to the end of humanity itself. Hawking, Koppel, and Musk have given us plenty to be afraid of.

Enter Vivos. Vivos is a company that transforms Cold War–era underground nuclear facilities into subterranean condominiums that are, according to the company's website, "built and engineered to withstand or mitigate just about everything from a pole shift, to super volcano eruptions, solar flares, earthquakes, tsunamis, pandemics, asteroid strikes, the anticipated effects of Planet X/Nibiru, and manmade threats including nuclear explosions, a reactor meltdown, biological or chemical disasters, terrorism and even widespread anarchy"! One of these facilities is in my home state of Kansas, and you can own a floor of it, well belowground, for a cool $3 million. The company offers "life assurance for a dangerous world." Who buys these units? They seem to be wealthy people who are willing to spend outrageous sums of money, "just in case."

ANTICIPATING THE WORST-CASE SCENARIO

There are reasonable, intelligent people who evaluate and seek to protect us from likely possible threats. This can be one of the "good gifts" of fear we spoke of earlier—anticipating worst-case scenarios and reacting accordingly to protect ourselves and others from them. At the same time, our fears about future threats can lead us into a quagmire of overreaction. Our fears can be preyed upon by charlatans seeking to make a buck; by politicians hoping to get elected; by causes hoping to receive funding; and by preachers hoping to literally scare the hell out of people.

Do you remember Y2K? The *Time* magazine cover in January 1999 captured well the feelings of many on the cusp of the new millennium. It showed a robed figure—a prophet or a messiah—wearing a sandwich board and holding a cross. The sign asked, "The End of the World!?! . . . Will computers melt down? Will society?" A crosswalk sign offered two messages: "Panic/Don't Panic." In addition to the hysteria that seems to accompany any major date change—the move into a new millennium being the biggest date change in a thousand years—there was a concern raised about our computer systems and how they would handle the change from 1999 to 2000.

The fear of what might happen led governments, businesses, and computer programmers to get to work analyzing the problem and developing solutions. Meanwhile, the imagination of the general public, fearmongers, the media, and religious leaders began to paint apocalyptic scenarios. Computers would stop working, the electric grid would shut down, banks and

ATMs would not function, and airplanes, with their onboard computers, would cease to fly and fall out of the sky. One well-known preacher even encouraged his flock to buy guns in the event of a revolution (so much for "love your enemy" and "turn the other cheek"!).

What happened when the clock turned over to January 1, 2000? Nearly nothing. The governments of countries that spent little, if anything, to address the issue continued without a hitch. Planes did not fall from the sky. Jesus did not return in the following months. There were, however, millions of people who had cases of drinking water and food and new gas generators taking up space in their garages.

Of course, we shouldn't blithely skip through life thinking only happy thoughts. Some challenges we face today are truly daunting on a global scale. But the cries of "the end of the world as we know it," while dismissed by the unconvinced, can breed fear and hysteria in some people. The greatest fear and threat to the human race for many today is global warming, with its predictions of melted polar ice caps, flooded coastlines, and major temperature shifts across the globe. For others, typically those on the opposite end of the ideological divide, the biggest fear is the loss of freedom, and a government that seems to control nearly every aspect of life.

GROWING UP ON TWO SIDES OF THE SAME THREAT

When I was growing up, our greatest fear wasn't the environment or computer bugs or government overreach; the existential enemy that threatened to destroy the world was the Soviet Union. Of course, to the Soviets, *the United States* was the supreme threat to civilization. Combined, those two nations built enough nuclear weapons to destroy each other and our allies many times over. Some readers will remember the civil defense drills in which children were either taken to a specially designed shelter or taught to "duck and cover" under their desks in the event of a nuclear attack.

Several years after the fall of the Soviet Union, I was in Moscow with a small group of leaders from my church, meeting and developing relationships with Christians of newly forming United Methodist churches in Russia. I remember walking with a woman my age at night at the newly opened Museum of the Great Patriotic War (this is the name Russians use for World War II). As we walked past the fountains and reflecting pool, red lights within the pool served as a reminder of the blood of the 8.7 million Russian soldiers who died in the war.

Both my friend and I were born nearly twenty years after the war. We shared so much in common. Both of us had experienced the duck-and-cover drills in our schools. We were both taught that the other's country was a very real threat to our way of life. We both anticipated war when we were growing up. As we talked that night, both of us wondered how we could possibly have considered killing the other in war.

In 1982, the year I graduated from high school, the Cold War reached a crisis level not seen since the early 1960s. President Reagan's tough talk about the "evil empire," when coupled with the pursuit of strategic defenses that might tilt the balance of power in favor of the United States, left some in the Soviet Union believing that America was preparing for war. The Soviet fear of the United States and NATO, and the US fear of the Soviet Union, brought the world close to nuclear war.*

---

* Robert Beckhusen, "New Documents Reveal How a 1980s Nuclear War Scare Became a Full-Blown Crisis," *Wired,* May 16, 2013.

I had just begun my second year of college on August 31, 1983, when Korean Airlines Flight 007, a Boeing 747 carrying 269 passengers and crew, took off from New York. It landed in Anchorage for refueling on its way to Seoul. After departing Anchorage, the plane veered slightly off course, entering Soviet airspace. The Soviets, assuming the United States was using a commercial plane in order to spy on military installations, instructed a Soviet Su-15 interceptor to destroy the plane, which it did, killing everyone on board. Among the passengers was a US congressman, Larry McDonald of Georgia. The incident took the United States and the Soviet Union one step closer to war. Every night for weeks this story dominated the news. I remember feeling then, and for the next few years, that nuclear war was inevitable.

Several months later, ABC broadcast a made-for-television film called *The Day After,* about a nuclear attack by the Soviets on the United States. Interestingly, the fictional attack targeted Kansas City, Missouri; Lawrence, Kansas; and rural missile silos in Kansas. I was in college, but the film, the most-watched television movie in history to that point, gave one hundred million viewers in America a picture of what a nuclear attack would look like. There is some evidence that this film led to a determination in America, and later in the Soviet Union (it was shown there to the public in 1987), to de-escalate the saber rattling and to work toward an intermediate-range nuclear weapons treaty.

STARTING WITH A BIAS OF HOPE

Fear of the other nearly led us to war, but fear of war and its effects walked us back from the brink. As we've learned, fear can be a good gift if it leads us to address real threats in helpful ways. But it can also be devastating when it is exaggerated, uninformed, or used by others to manipulate us.

Here's the point, in case you've missed it amid these historical anecdotes: In nearly every age, human beings have lived in dread of enemies, apocalyptic visions, and potential catastrophes that might come upon us, either from the gods, from the devil, from nature, or from our enemies. Some of these fears had a foundation in facts and represented very real possibilities. But despite two thousand years of possible Armageddon, the human race is still here. Sometimes our fears saved us as we got to work to solve great problems; sometimes our fears were overblown and nearly destroyed us.

Living unafraid despite the possible dangers we face as a race does not require a $3 million investment in a luxury bomb shelter. It simply comes down to our acronym:

Face your fears with faith.
Examine your assumptions in light of the facts.
Attack your anxieties with action.
Release your cares to God.

Facing our fears with *faith* means starting with a bias of hope. This is not only faith in God but faith in modern science's ability to find solutions or alternatives, or faith in our fellow human beings or our institutions. We *examine our assumptions* that are frightening us in light of the facts. So often those of us on both the left and the right will hear of a possible threat that aligns with our biases, and we immediately accept it as fact, rather than digging deeper by looking to subject-matter experts (in the case of the Y2K scare, the experts were right, while the fearmongers got it all wrong). *Attacking our anxieties with action* means doing what we can do to address our fears or to be a part of the solution and not the problem. Are you fearful about global warming? Take action to do your part to reduce your carbon footprint. (Action helps ameliorate fear.) And, ultimately, release your fears to God.

WHAT CAN I PERSONALLY DO?

Above I've raised a host of possible fears, from nuclear war to artificial intelligence taking over the world to global warming. Like terrorism, these are serious issues that do (or in the case of AI could) threaten our existence. The pileup of potential apocalypses can be paralyzing, which is why I recommend proceeding thoughtfully, practically, and—maybe most important—with a hope that we can find a solution. In this spirit, I seek to know all I can about the real nature of the threat, including reading voices from opposing sides of the issue or concern and their assessments of the problem and possible solutions. I ask myself what I can do personally to be a part of the solution. When it comes to global warming, for example, I can address the issue in intentional ways, pursuing a more environmentally responsible lifestyle. Ultimately, once I've done all I can to understand and act, I trust in God.

I remember how real the threat of war appeared in 1982–83. I wasn't terrified, but it did seem a very real possibility at the time. And fear was an appropriate response for anyone who understood the gravity of the situation. I wanted to live, despite this fear, unafraid. I remember finding comfort in the words of the final book of the Bible, Revelation. Mine was not the comfort drawn from those who see Revelation as a road map to the End Times. Most scholars, in fact, don't view Revelation in this way, but instead as a letter written to the Christians of what is today eastern Turkey to encourage them to remain steadfast, to not compromise with the culture around them, and to know that even if they were persecuted or put to death, God would ultimately prevail.

ENDING WITH PARADISE RESTORED

Revelation ends by taking readers back to the Garden of Eden, where the Bible begins. It paints a picture of the climax of human history. In the end, Eden is restored.

> *Then I saw a new heaven and a new earth, for the former heaven and the former earth had passed away, and the sea was no more. I saw the holy city, New Jerusalem, coming down out of heaven from God, made ready as a bride beautifully dressed for her husband. I heard a loud voice from the throne say, "Look! God's dwelling is here with humankind. He will dwell with them, and they will be his peoples. God himself will be with them as their God. He will wipe away every tear from their eyes. Death will be no more. There will be no mourning, crying, or pain anymore, for the former things have passed away."*
>
> (REVELATION 21:1–4)

These words reminded me then, as now, that the biblical message is that the dystopian visions we have, and the dystopian realities we sometimes experience, will never have the final word. Though paradise was lost in the opening chapters of the Bible, the Bible ends with paradise restored. In the end, God, goodness, love, and life will ultimately prevail, even if, for a time, evil, destruction, and death seem to have the upper hand.

Or, as Handel so magnificently put it, one day, "the kingdom of this world is become the kingdom of our Lord, and of his Christ and he shall reign forever and ever."

This hope is not meant to lead us to apathy or indifference about the very real problems facing our world. The Bible calls human beings to work to address the world's problems. But we do so as people who have hope that regardless of what happens, ultimately, God will prevail.

ABOVEGROUND WORKING AND SERVING

Because I believe that God will prevail despite our best efforts to destroy ourselves, I don't need to have a luxury bunker deep underground in the event of an apocalypse. If some cataclysm is coming, I'd rather be aboveground working, serving, and if necessary dying, alongside my friends and family and fellow human beings.

I love how Israel's prophets nearly all noted that despite the apocalyptic destruction Israel would one day experience at the hands of neighboring empires, ultimately God would deliver his people. In the light of this promise, the prophet Zechariah called the Jewish people "prisoners of hope" (Zechariah 9:12). No matter how frightening the future seems, or how terrifying the past may have been, God is still God, you are God's people, and there is ALWAYS hope. The scriptures don't lead us to indifference to the dangers and threats in our world today. But they do show us how to respond to these fears with courage and hope.

14

We Never Did It That Way Before

Time isn't the enemy. Fear of change is.

— Oprah Winfrey

While we may feel miserable, unvalued, unappreciated, and unchallenged in our jobs, there is often a level of comfort in this misery—it is the devil we know.

—Zoë Wundenberg

Human beings are change-averse. The fear of change keeps some people in miserable marriages, and others from ever getting married at all, even when they are deeply in love. The fear of change motivates some to stay in jobs they can't stand, and others to say no to jobs that would have brought them great joy. I was not surprised when the Egyptian human rights activist Amr Hamzawy said that the fear of change kept millions in the Arab world living under authoritarian regimes.* As the familiar saying goes, "Better the devil you know than the devil you don't know."

Many of the other fears we've studied are close partners with the fear of change—the fear of failure and the fear of

---

* "Fear of Change," *Qantara*, July 26, 2017, https://en.qantara.de/content /authoritarian-rule-in-the-arab-world-fear-of-change.

disappointing others, to name just two. With some regularity, I've led our congregation through the process of change, but there's a part of me that always dreads it, knowing that even very modest changes can bring complaints and cause people to leave the church. I know of churches that would rather die than change, and leaders who would rather let their churches die than have to take the heat for leading their congregations to essential changes.

When I was younger, and the church was smaller, I greeted change with enthusiasm. I loved the challenge and had fun casting vision and leading us to a change that I knew would result in new opportunities for ministry and the chance to reach more people. But as the church grew, change became harder. The larger any organization becomes, the harder it is to change, and the more the stakeholders tend to offer some version of "We never did it that way before." Sometimes the older we get, the more we dread change.

LEADING THE WAY AT EIGHTY

But it's not always true that being younger makes us less fearful of or less resistant to change, or that the older we are the more fearful and resistant we become. Several months ago, I was invited to have lunch at one of the large retirement communities near the church. The residents had hooked up an Apple TV and a projector so that they could tap into our online worship services, effectively starting a new satellite church on their own—a community of people whose average age is eighty did this! While at lunch, they began to tell me about how diverse their community is, and that it includes even gay and lesbian couples, and how grateful they are for these couples. These eighty-year-olds had accepted gay couples while people I know in their forties and fifties struggle to do so. Sometimes it's the older adults who lead the way.

Likewise, even young adults can be fearful of change. I know young adults who are afraid to go off to college. Part of the issue is a kind of separation anxiety, but there's also a fear of the unknown. The fear of growing up is a real thing—at the clinical level it is called gerascophobia. In 2016, a group of researchers in America studied the fear of maturity among college undergraduates. They reviewed responses to questions administered to students in 1982, 1992, 2002, and 2012. The research revealed that young adults today, in the words of the title of the report, "don't want to grow up."*

As with most of the other fears we've considered, the problem isn't that we feel some fear or anxiety about change—it's normal and even healthy to feel some anxiety about doing things differently than you've done them before. The problem arises when our fears control us and we give in to them and find ourselves paralyzed or stuck.

Now, there are times when we need to listen to our fears. Sometimes those anxieties or worries are a warning sign that something isn't right. But often, giving in to our fear of change leaves us missing out on a better life, more joy, or some grand adventure. Sometimes giving in to the fear of change means watching our business or organization die a slow death. It means missing the opportunity of a lifetime, or just an important turn we should have taken.

---

* April Smith, Lindsay P. Bodell, Jill Holm-Denoma, Thomas Joiner, Kathryn Gordon, Marisol Perez, and Pamela Keel, "I Don't Want to Grow Up, I'm a [Gen X, Y, Me] Kid," *International Journal of Behavioral Development*, June 21, 2016, http://journals.sagepub.com/doi/abs /10.1177/0165025416654302.

WAITING FOR THE PERFECT MOMENT

When I think of the impact our fear of change can have on us, I think of a story in the Gospel of John. It takes place at the Pool of Bethesda (alternatively known as the Pool of Bethsaida) in Jerusalem. It was believed that from time to time the waters were stirred by angels, and that the first person into the water following its stirring would be healed. In hope of finding healing, sick people gathered near the pool to wait.

John writes, "A certain man was there who had been sick for thirty-eight years. When Jesus saw him lying there, knowing that he had already been there a long time, he asked him, 'Do you want to get well?' The sick man answered him, 'Sir, I don't have anyone who can put me in the water when it is stirred up. When I'm trying to get to it, someone else has gotten in ahead of me' " (5:5–7). Jesus goes on to heal the man.

Two things stand out to me in the story: First, the man had been at this pool for thirty-eight years. Although he was sick, somehow he managed to get himself to the pool each day, but in all of those years why hadn't he ever been able to get into the water? The second is Jesus's question "Do you want to get well?" What kind of question is that? Unless, of course, the man had never managed to get into the water because he was afraid. Perhaps the cause of his paralysis was the fear of what his life would be like if he were ever not sick.

It is easy to become comfortable with the misery we know and, though we might have a way out, fearful of what this change could mean for us.

I recall a woman who became anxious when her alcoholic husband began attending AA. She knew how to live with her husband the drinker. It was an unhealthy relationship, but it was familiar. She was really afraid of who her husband would be if he ever stopped drinking. And, in fact, her marriage did not survive her husband's becoming healthy. It was going to require changes from her that she was unwilling to make.

Broader societal and technological changes can leave many of us disoriented, anxious, and afraid. I remember when the Internet first became accessible on a widespread basis. I was speaking with a woman who, at the time, was in her thirties. She told me she would never hook her computer up to the Internet, not only because she felt the content was dangerous but because others could find her and perhaps steal her data. Today she's a regular user, but it took years after most people had logged on before she joined in.

With sociological and technological changes can come another closely related fear—the fear of becoming obsolete. We recently had a panel of millennial staff members at the church, most of them in their late twenties and early thirties, speak to the rest of our team. They were describing what was important to people their age and helping us understand the differences between baby boomers and gen Xers and their own generation, the millennials (also known as generation Y). I know that some of our staff were feeling a bit obsolete. Several weeks later, I was sitting at a conference listening to a panel of teenage girls describe how their generation, Z, differed from the millennials. Now some of the gen Yers in the audience were themselves feeling obsolete!

Has fear of change ever paralyzed you in any way? Consider once more our acronym: face your fears with faith, examine your assumptions in light of the facts, attack your anxieties with action, and release your fears to God. These simple but effective steps can put you in motion toward hope and healing.

"DAD, I'M NOT DYING. I'M JUST MOVING TO KANSAS STATE"

Only recently have I come to understand another hidden emotional dynamic that can amplify our fear of change: grief over what we're leaving behind. Not long ago, my senior leadership team and I met with Craig Peterson, the vice president of organizational development at a large company in Kansas City who has focused on change management. He explained that the model he uses to help companies work through change was built in part on Elisabeth Kübler-Ross's well-known findings about grief. Craig's model recognizes that change means a kind of "death" to what was familiar, comfortable, known, and often loved. The fear of change, he recognized, is often the result of anticipatory grief.

As I listened to Craig, a vivid memory came to mind: the night before our oldest daughter moved to college. I knelt next to her bed to pray for her, as I had done pretty much every night since she was born. As I started to pray, I quickly began to weep. After a moment, Danielle gently said, "Dad, I'm not dying. I'm just moving to Kansas State."

We laugh about it now, but that's the moment it dawned on me that Danielle and I faced endings of a very different kind. She was leaving friends and the comforts of home and that was sad, but the excitement of college and beginning the next chapter in her life more than offset any sadness she was feeling. But for me, I was grieving the ending of a part of my life I so very much enjoyed. After our second (and last) daughter moved away, I went through a six-month season of grief. I would come home from work and neither girl was home to greet me. I would look upstairs at night and there were no lights on in their rooms. No more supper conversations with the girls. It was terribly hard for both LaVon and me. And at the same time we were grateful that our kids had grown up and were independent.

NEW JOYS ON THE OTHER SIDE

But then, in the midst of this terribly painful season of change, we began to discover new joys. LaVon and I had a freedom we'd not known in twenty-two years. We also found that when the kids came home we had really wonderful grown-up conversations. Then our oldest got married, and that was another source of great joy. Our youngest lives in New York, and her moving so far away was hard. But now we take trips to see her, she comes back to Kansas City regularly, and we enjoy family vacations more now than ever. Several years ago we had our first granddaughter, and we discovered the amazing joy of being grandparents—an incomparable joy that I could not possibly have imagined that night as I wept at Danielle's bedside.

Yes, change is hard and frightening. It's frightening because we're used to doing things a certain way—we know how to do this—and we don't want to lose what is comfortable and familiar. Change means learning new things, doing things in new ways, and taking risks without the assurance of success. No wonder we so often keep doing the same things, even when we don't like the results.

But change is rarely as hard as we fear it will be. We don't need to let our fears leave us stranded, paralyzed for years at our own Pool of Bethesda. Faith in God, faith in the future, faith that we can adapt and grow and survive—this faith gives us the capacity to say yes to change. And as I've personally discovered, what often waits for us on the other side of change is joy.

15

FOMO

FOMO *n. [Fear of Missing Out] anxiety that an exciting or interesting event may currently be happening else-where, often aroused by posts seen on social media.*

—*New Oxford American Dictionary*

FOMO, OR THE FEAR OF MISSING OUT, MIGHT BE ONE OF the trendier expressions on social media, but the phenomenon is not new. It's probably been around as long as humans. I imagine the caveman, upon hearing his neighbor grunt and head out with a club to hunt, grabbing his own club and following for fear of missing out. In biblical times they called it "coveting." More recently, we call it "keeping up with the Joneses"—the longing not only for the material things your neighbors own but to do whatever seemingly pleasurable or fashionable thing they are doing.

FOMO is all of those things on steroids. When I was a kid, I used to look across the street and imagine the wonderful things the rich kid's family in my neighborhood was doing. But now we don't have to imagine; we can see it all in real time on social media. FOMO can strike every time a neighbor or friend posts pictures of their amazing vacation, the really cool birthday party they had (to which I wasn't invited), the awesome places they eat, and the conversations they have with all the cool people they interact with on Facebook, Instagram, and Twitter. If I'm not reasonably secure and happy myself, looking at all those posts with their pics of the happiness, bliss, and just plain awesomeness of everyone else's life can make me anxious, insecure, and unhappy.

THE PANG OF MISSING SOMETHING BETTER

FOMO was first named in *The Harbus*—the Harvard Business School's independent newspaper—on May 10, 2004. The author of the piece, HBS student Patrick McGinnis, actually named two related conditions. One was FOMO. The other was FOBO, or fear of a better offer. McGinnis offered his acronyms tongue in cheek, but I suspect you've felt the very real pang of both at some point.

In McGinnis's story, FOMO led one presumably fictional Harvard student to schedule a night of multiple meet-ups with different friends for drinks every fifty minutes or so until the wee hours of the morning. No way was he going to miss out on the fun anyone else was having, and his neurotic evening plans proved it.

But then, before his big evening, he received an e-mail from another friend, who offered him the chance to go to a Red Sox game followed by a party. Tragically, he had already confirmed plans with all of the people he was scheduled to meet up with, and he was too embarrassed to cancel his dates. So he missed an even better offer, all because he had planned one day too soon. From that time on, this Harvard student suffered from FOBO—fear of a better offer, the close companion of FOMO. This led him to always be tentative in making plans so that he would be free to abandon them in the event a better offer came along!*

The story might have been satirical, but the phenomenon is very real. My wife and I were on vacation in California with friends, and I had two weeks left to finish the first draft of this book. It was nearly finished, but I'd set aside one day for writing. LaVon and our friends said, "Great, you stay here and write—we're heading to the town of Sonoma." Then it happened. Our friends started talking about their previous visit to Sonoma—this great restaurant they'd been to, and a wonderful little winery—and pretty soon I came down with a full-blown case of FOMO. My publisher could wait another day. I couldn't stand the thought of missing out!

By the way, FOMO is not restricted to college students or married couples on vacation. The common midlife crisis is another expression of the fear of missing out. At middle age, we realize we have fewer good years ahead of us than behind us, and we become afraid that we're missing out. I've had a half-dozen men, and a few women, in my office over the last thirty years who described the fears that led them to cheat on their spouses.

THE PERFECT ANXIETY-PRODUCING MACHINE

Social media helped to promote FOMO from a term in an obscure satirical article in a Harvard paper to a clinical state of anxiety most people under thirty are familiar with and feel they have suffered from at some point.

---

* The Harbus [Patrick McGinnis], "Social Theory at HBS: McGinnis' Two FO's," *The Harbus,* May 10, 2004, http://www.harbus.org/2004/social-theory-at-hbs-2749/.

The great thing about social media is the way it keeps you connected with people with whom you might not otherwise remain in contact. You can follow them, peering into the best moments of their lives. And they can do the same with you.

But all of this can come at a price to your mental health. I remember hearing a conversation a few years ago on National Public Radio with several teenage girls. They were reporting on their use of social media and the feelings they had when they posted something and only a few people responded. They described the feelings of rejection when they had fewer friends than others or if someone unfriended them or refused to accept their friend request, and how they felt when they saw that a friend was doing something without including them. Social media has become the perfect machine for producing anxiety.

If you've felt yourself afflicted by social media–induced anxiety, it's good to remember a few basic things about posts— things you likely already know but sometimes forget. I think my own posting habits are pretty typical of what most of us do on social media, and I've noticed that certain unstated "rules" apply, or should. When I post a photo online, it is never of my wife and me fighting, or when I'm not feeling good, or when my life is just ordinary and boring. I also avoid posting pictures that make me look fatter or older than I really am. I've been known to crop a picture a bit before posting just because the original seems to add twenty pounds or accentuates the crow's-feet around my eyes. What does this mean? It means that if you see my pictures on Facebook, Twitter, or Instagram* you should know that you are seeing only my best, happiest moments

---

* https://www.facebook.com/PastorAdamHamilton; @RevAdamHamilton on Twitter; and revadamhamilton on Instagram, though I don't post there often!

and these do not reflect my entire life, just the particularly good times.

Not long ago I was with friends who had been bickering. By the end of the day, they could barely stand to sit together. But at one point they had a picture taken against a beautiful backdrop. They smiled for the photo and then turned away from each other right after it was taken. They eventually got over their irritation with each other, but when the photo turned up on Facebook not long after, I had to smile. They looked so happy and in love in that picture, but I knew, because I was there, that just before it was taken, they were contemplating divorce! One way of addressing FOMO in your life is to remember that what you see on social media posts isn't reality, but the small slice of life someone wants to allow others to share.

A second way to address FOMO is to take a break from social media, or at least ratchet down your use. For many people, social media is an addiction—our brains crave it the moment we get up in the morning, and we need it again on each break at work. We look at it while we're shopping, eating, with other friends, even in the bathroom. And then, just before we go to bed, we check it once more, going to sleep with images in our mind of the awesome life everyone else is living!

If FOMO has you down, try taking a break for a week, a month, or maybe even a year. I've met a surprising number of people who are doing just that. When we're constantly on social media and looking at what other people are doing in their lives, we fail to live in the moment in the life we're actually living.*

---

* For actual research into this effect, check out "The Facebook Experiment," published by the Happiness Research Institute and found at: https://docs.wixstatic.com/ugd/928487_680fc12644c8428eb728cde7d61b13e7.pdf.

WHAT WOULD JESUS POST?

Whenever you post on social media, you might want to think carefully about how your post could affect others. This falls in the category of Jesus's advice to "do unto others as you would have them do unto you." I seldom post pictures of things I'm doing with my friends, and I rarely mention them because I don't want others to feel left out. If I post a photo, it will be with my family or of a place. It is worth asking, "Why am I posting this photo (or story or meme)?" Is it to impress others? To make myself look good? We find our fear of missing out is fed by social media, but we can also feed others' FOMO with our posts.

Nearly every expert I've read on happiness has noted that it's counterproductive to focus on what others have that you don't have, or what others are doing that you are not doing. This only creates envy and unhappiness. And interestingly, even if you do manage to do the things others are doing and have the things other have, it seldom leads to happiness.

The ancient Greeks had a word for happiness—*eudaimonia*—yet the word meant more than mere happiness. It encompassed being blessed, flourishing, experiencing well-being, and feeling joyful—in other words, the good life. But the Greeks wrestled, as we do, with how to achieve the good life. For many, the pursuit of happiness gets reduced to hedonism—a philosophy that seeks to maximize pleasure while minimizing pain.

The writer of Ecclesiastes famously pursued this philosophy for a time. We can't be sure who wrote the book, though he is traditionally identified as King Solomon. He describes his experience as follows:

I built houses and planted vineyards for myself; I made myself gardens and parks, and planted in them all kinds

*of fruit trees. I made myself pools from which to water the
forest of growing trees. . . . I also had great possessions of
herds and flocks, more than any who had been before me
in Jerusalem. I also gathered for myself silver and gold
and the treasure of kings and of the provinces; I got singers, both men and women, and delights of the flesh, and
many concubines. So I became great and surpassed all
who were before me in Jerusalem. . . . Whatever my eyes
desired I did not keep from them; I kept my heart from
no pleasure.*

(ECCLESIASTES 2, MISCELLANEOUS VERSES)

The Bible describes Solomon's wealth, his palaces and
horses, and 1 Kings 11:3 even notes that "among his wives were
seven hundred princesses and three hundred concubines." Talk
about being motivated by a fear of missing out! Yet for all his
pursuit of pleasure, near the end of his life he wrote, "I considered all that my hands had done and the toil I had spent in
doing it, and again, all was vanity and a chasing after wind"
(Ecclesiastes 2:11). The word translated here as "vanity" is ren-
dered in other versions as "meaningless."

Psychologists have a name for what happened to the author of the book of Ecclesiastes—hedonic adaptation. You buy
something—a new phone, purse, watch, pair of shoes, car,
house—but even if you've been dreaming about it for ages, the
joy your new purchase brings diminishes quickly. Before long,
you are already thinking about the next purchase that will
make you happy.

RETRAINING YOUR MIND FOR HAPPINESS

Greek and Roman philosophers proposed that retraining your mind was central to happiness and defeating the restless heart syndrome we call hedonism. They said we should learn to *want what we already have, not what we don't yet have*. Interestingly, they taught that the way to accomplish this retraining was to cultivate gratitude—an ethic that is central to the Bible.

In his book *A Guide to the Good Life: The Ancient Art of Stoic Joy*, William B. Irvine notes that this is the power of saying grace before a meal. You stop three times a day to give thanks for what you have—even if your meal is a bowl of porridge. You count your blessings. You thank God for the food before you, for the hands that prepared it, for life, for the people with whom you share it. I've found that in my marriage, giving thanks for my wife every night before I go to bed, and actually stopping to thank her and tell her how grateful I am for her, makes me happier in our marriage. The alternative—focusing on what frustrates us about the other and imagining how much happier we'd be if we were married to someone else—would have led to divorce years ago.

This is what Paul had in mind when in 1 Thessalonians 5:16 he wrote, "Rejoice always. Pray continually. Give thanks in every situation because this is God's will for you in Christ Jesus." I love this verse because it succinctly offers a picture of the good life and how we obtain it. How can we rejoice always? By praying continually—communing with God in prayer. And what do we say? We say, "Thank you."

Robert Emmons, considered to be the leading scientific expert on gratitude, has devoted much of his career at the University of California, Davis, to studying the connection between gratitude and happiness. His research found that regularly expressing gratitude makes people happier, more fulfilled, and more likely to flourish. Gratitude also positively affects our physical and emotional health, and our relationships with others.

The writer of Ecclesiastes concluded his report on his FOMO-induced excesses with these words: "So this is the end of the matter; all has been heard. Worship God and keep God's commandments" (12:13). In other words, he found that the pursuit of happiness failed to make him happy. But doing God's will and giving thanks to God actually brought contentment and satisfaction. So, the next time you pick up your phone or open up your tablet or computer and start feeling envious over your friends' latest posts, tweets, or pictures, remember that you're looking at only the best moments from what is likely an otherwise pretty ordinary life. Look for the blessings in your own life, giving thanks for what you have. Worship God in word and deed, and you'll already be experiencing what Saint Paul calls "the life that really is life."

16

I Could Buy Me a Boat

Dogs have no money. Isn't that amazing? They're broke their entire lives. But they get through. You know why dogs have no money? No pockets.

—JERRY SEINFELD

Do not worry about your life, what you will eat or what you will drink; or about your body, what you will wear. . . . Consider the lilies of the field, how they grow; they neither toil nor spin, yet I tell you, even Solomon in all his glory was not clothed like one of these.

—JESUS

LAST SUMMER, AS I WAS WORKING THROUGH THE MATERIAL for this chapter, friends from Texas joined LaVon and me for a weekend at the Lake of the Ozarks. Just for the occasion, one of them created a playlist on his iPad that he titled "Lake Music." The song that quickly became our favorite was "Buy Me a Boat" by Chris Janson. In the country-and-western hit, Janson dreams about what it would be like to be wealthy and what he'd buy with the money if he had it. Sure, being rich wouldn't fix everything. But still, as the song's refrain declares:

Money can't buy everything.
Well, maybe so,
But it could buy me a boat.

Janson goes on to say that it could buy him a truck, a trailer, a Yeti cooler, and plenty of beer. The first time I heard "Buy Me a Boat" I burst out laughing. It so perfectly captures how many people feel about money. Can you relate? Sure, money won't fix everything. And yes, it gets a lot of folks in trouble. But then again, if you had just a bit more perhaps you could kiss all those financial stresses and strains good-bye. And . . . you could have that boat!

According to a recent survey conducted by the American Psychological Association, money is the number one source of stress for Americans. This is true not only for lower-income people but also for middle-income and, perhaps surprisingly, high-income people. Even millionaires worry about financial security. The Swiss financial firm UBS conducted a survey not long ago of 2,215 US investors with a net worth of at least $1 million. More than 600 of them had a net worth in excess of $5 million. Of those millionaires who were millennials, half said they were somewhat or very afraid of losing their wealth.

When the millionaires were asked, "About how much wealth do you aspire to eventually have?," not surprisingly, the wealthier the respondent was, the higher the reported financial goal: "Those with $1 million want $2 million; those with $10 million want $25 million."

All that money didn't seem to garner them much security either. Sixty-three percent noted that "one major setback (e.g., lost job, market crash) would have a major impact on my lifestyle," and more than half reported that they "sometimes feel stuck on a treadmill."[*]

LaVon and I began our married life living just below the poverty level for a family of two in 1982. I was attending college and working part-time. She worked full-time at an entry-level job with General Motors. We lived in a rough part of town and furnished our home with stuff we'd either bought at garage sales or picked up on the side of the street for free after the garage sale was over. Even after our income rose above the poverty level, we still lived paycheck to paycheck. One year, when the engine went bad on our Ford Tempo, I sold my 1950s and 1960s baseball card collection to pay for car repairs (how I regret that now!).

By our thirties, we were beginning to earn enough to make ends meet. We had two kids, a couple of car payments, and we had followed our real estate agent's advice to buy "as much house as you can qualify for." All of this meant that even though we were making more money than we made in our twenties, our lifestyle had risen with our income, and once more we got to the end of the year asking, "Where did all of it go?" Now, though we no longer live paycheck to paycheck, we still ask this question each year as we do our taxes: "What happened to all the money we made last year?" But today we also ask two other questions: Will we have enough for retirement? What happens to our family if I, as the primary breadwinner, become injured or incapacitated or die?

---

[*] Investor Watch Treadmill, http://view.ceros.com/ubs/investor-watch -treadmill/p/2.

DESIRE, DISCIPLINE, AND FINANCIAL DISTRESS

In my experience, two very human factors—desire and lack of discipline—determine whether an individual or a family can live within their means. If we don't deal with these thoughtfully and persistently, we're likely to slide into financial distress, and even if we earn enough to avoid distress, we're likely to find that we've squandered much of what we have, missing out on even more important or meaningful things we might have done with our resources.

Let's think about desire for a moment. We live in an economy based on consumer spending. In order for consumers to spend they must be convinced that they need more, or that what they have is somehow inadequate. This is why advertisers constantly bombard us with messages that tell us we'd be happier if we just had a bit more. If only we had a boat, and a truck to pull it, and a Yeti 110 cooler, as Chris Janson sings, we'd finally be happy.

It's funny, before listening to "Buy Me a Boat," I had never heard of a Yeti cooler. But after hearing Janson extol its virtues, I went to the company website and read the description. They are amazing coolers. They keep their contents cold for days at a time, and they're also practically indestructible. Bears can't even break into them. I was hooked.

"Vonnie, we need a Yeti!" I told my wife.

"What's a Yeti?" she said.

"It's a cooler that is amazing. It will keep stuff cool for days, and the 110-quart is only $499!"

"You've got to be crazy."

"But, honey, it is certified bear-resistant!" Never mind that the only bears in Kansas City live at the zoo.

I think about the boat in Chris Janson's song. If you've ever owned a boat you know that most people who buy a boat—within a few years, months, or sometimes just days after they buy it—want a bigger boat. The same is often true when you buy a truck. That's the principle of hedonic adaptation that we talked about in the last chapter.

"BE ON YOUR GUARD"

On this topic I find Jesus's words to be so powerful and instructive. In Luke's Gospel Jesus says, "Be on your guard against all kinds of greed; for one's life does not consist in the abundance of possessions" (12:15). That verse has had a profound impact on my life. So often we take for granted our culture's suggestion that our lives *do* consist of the abundance of possessions. We charge up our credit cards and go into debt believing that if we had just a little bit more we'd finally be happy, believing our lives consist of the things we own. When this desire becomes the focus of our lives, or when we stop exercising restraint and self-discipline in response to it, that's when we get into trouble.

Many of us struggle with both discipline and desire when it comes to spending—and the numbers from financial experts prove it. A savings rule of thumb tells us we should be saving 10 to 15 percent of our income, but according to the Bureau of Economic Analysis, the average wage earner saves less than 5 percent. Half of all American households have recurring credit card debt, and the average household that maintains credit card debt has over $16,000 worth.* (Let's not miss the good news that half of all American households do not have

---

* Erin El Issa, "2016 American Household Credit Card Debt Study," NerdWallet.com, https://www.nerdwallet.com/blog/credit-card-data/average -credit-card-debt-household/.

any credit card debt—if they use credit cards they pay them off each month.) Student loan debt, however, is now the highest in history, exceeding $35,000 for each student who borrows to go to college.

What about giving? Most Americans who identify as Jewish or Christian (that's 72 percent)* know of the biblical call to give the first 10 percent of what we have to God and God's work. Interestingly, charitable giving as a percentage of adjusted gross income (AGI) declines the more money we make up to $1 million per year, then increases. So, according to IRS filings, people with an AGI of $50,000 to $75,000 per year give away 4.8 percent of their income, but those making between $500,000 and $1 million a year give away 2.8 percent of their income on average.** Why does the percentage of giving decline the more money we make?

Perhaps not surprisingly, older adults who grew up during the Depression did much better than my generation in practicing financial self-discipline. And among millennials, we're seeing more responsible attitudes toward spending, saving, and stewardship as well. Growing up in harder financial times might explain this. Millennials entered adulthood during the Great Recession, graduating from high school or college at a time of high unemployment for their age group. Aside from racking up too much college debt, they have stayed away from credit cards—a 2014 study found that 63 percent of millennials have *no* credit cards. That's awesome. On the down side, they do have debit cards, which, unfortunately, are more likely to incur late or overdraft charges, and millennials make late

---

* "Religious Landscape Study," Pew Research Center, http://www.pew forum.org/religious-landscape-study/.

** These numbers are reported by the IRS for the 2014 tax year.

payments at a rate almost twice that of baby boomers, thus incurring even higher finance charges due to late fees. Experian, a credit rating company, says that millennials' average FICO credit score is 628, which is below average and the lowest of all generations in America today.

LIVING BENEATH (IN A GOOD WAY)

Still, millennials can teach the rest of us a thing or two about money. The first is that, in much larger numbers than the two previous generations, they seek to *live beneath their means*. By not using credit cards and by avoiding buying things they cannot afford, they practice a principle that the financial adviser Dave Ramsey calls "acting your wage." And second, many millennials have adopted a mantra that previous generations didn't figure out: "Cheap is cool." Not all millennials by any means, but a significant subset shop at thrift stores and clothing exchanges. When I was a kid, this was a sign that your family struggled financially. Today it is a sign that you are hip. I've learned this from my daughter Rebecca, who loves to shop in thrift stores. I remember in high school she wanted to shop for her prom dress at the Salvation Army Thrift Store. I felt a bit embarrassed taking my daughter to shop there, but we ended up paying $20 for a designer dress, likely worn only once, that would've sold for more than $200 new. I suddenly realized she was brilliant.

What would it look like for *you* to live beneath your means? You already know the answer. It would look like less anxiety, less stress, less financial fear, more hope, and more financial freedom.

LaVon and I began practicing this as soon as our income rose above poverty level. We almost always purchase things that are two or three notches below what we can actually afford, which gives us margin, leaving us more money for giving and saving. Perhaps you are old enough to remember a book published in 1996 called *The Millionaire Next Door*. Two researchers studied persons with net worth in excess of $1 million ($1,560,000 in 2017 dollars). They found that a large number of millionaires were living in middle-class and blue-collar communities. These persons had amassed significant resources by means of fairly simple principles, including living beneath their means. They also placed little value on status objects or a status lifestyle. They didn't need the newest, latest, greatest. For example, because they bought good-condition used cars rather than new cars, they had money left over to save, invest, and give. Not surprisingly, they were saving, investing, and giving at much higher rates than those who spent nearly everything they had. And they had significantly less worry, fear, and anxiety related to money than those who spent more.

Are you living above, at, or below your means? There's nothing admirable or praiseworthy about spending more than you make. It doesn't make you happy—it makes you a slave.

"Therefore I tell you, do not worry about your life, what you will eat or what you will drink, or about your body, what you will wear. Is not life more than food, and the body more than clothing?" When Jesus spoke these words in his Sermon on the Mount (Matthew 6:25), he was likely writing both to people who were struggling to make ends meet and to people who were struggling for nicer things to wear and eat.

I love that last line: "Is not life more than food, and the body more than clothing?" This requires us to ask, "What is life really about?" Here, once again, millennials have something to teach us. Many of them live by the truth that life is found in *relationships, experiences,* and *serving,* not in possessions. I've seen this in my own children, who are far less concerned with having nice and expensive things, and much more interested in having meaningful experiences and relationships, and in making a difference in the world.

Each intentionally lives below her means. They live in more modest houses and drive more modest cars than others who earn their same income. They prefer playing games with their friends, or going to art shows, or sharing a meal with companions to taking expensive vacations (unless Mom and Dad are footing the bill!) and purchasing pricey things. And each is generous with her time and resources, giving to others and serving in some way. One of my daughters recently took a job paying half of what she could have made working elsewhere. She took the job, forgoing the higher income, because she saw it as a chance to help people.

My daughters are living what Jesus spoke of when he said, "Do not store up for yourselves treasures on earth, where moth and rust consume and where thieves break in and steal; but store up for yourselves treasures in heaven, where neither moth nor rust consumes and where thieves do not break in and steal. For where your treasure is, there your heart will be also" (Matthew 6:19–21).

THE RIGHT KIND OF FINANCIAL FEAR

"Where your treasure is, there your heart will be also." My mother taught me these words of Jesus when I was young— that how I spent my money said a lot about my priorities and what really mattered to me. This is part of why LaVon and I began giving away the first 10 percent of what we earn when were still in high school. When we married and lived at the poverty level, we continued to give the first 10 percent of what we earned. This was, for us, nonnegotiable. We lived on what was left. Looking back, we felt that God honored the fact that we had prioritized our giving. As our income has grown over the years, the percentage that we give away has increased as well. I don't believe that God is going to make you rich if you give. But in our lives, I do believe that God saw how, when we had nothing, we sought to be generous with what little we had, and God blessed that, and gave us greater opportunities and responsibilities. To this day, our first priority in spending every year is giving. Giving actually serves in some ways as an antidote to the perpetual desire for more.

Most of us will carry a measure of anxiety about money— and that fear can be a good thing if it motivates us to be careful about our spending. Paradoxically, the right kind of financial fear can lead us to establish a lifestyle that's simpler, more disciplined, and more focused on generosity. There are five basic financial principles that can help us to do that:

1. Develop and use a budget.
2. Avoid debt, using it only for your house, car, and education if you must.
3. Live at least two steps below your means.
4. Set a goal of giving away 10 percent or more of your income.
5. Save at least 10 percent of your income for the future.

That takes me back to Chris Janson's hit song "Buy Me a Boat." It sold over 1 million copies and launched his career. Yet despite the song's message, when *Billboard* magazine asked Chris about happiness, this is what he said: "Happiness means my family. That's off-kilter [relative to] the song, but happiness is my wife and kids, my faith and relationship with the Lord."

Billboard asked if the song made him a million bucks what he would do with it. Janson said, "If I ever make a million dollars with anything in life, I'm going to tell you like I told everyone else—and I mean this—I'm going to buy diapers first. As long as my family is set and secure with their livelihood, I'm happy. . . . Money can buy a boat, but I don't even know if I want a boat. . . . It's all about my wife and kids, man. Anything else is just icing on the cake."*

---

* Elias Leight, "Country Singer Chris Janson on Why He'll Buy Diapers with His First $1 Million," *Billboard,* June 23, 2015.

Part Five

AGING, ILLNESS, DYING, AND FEAR OF THE LORD

INTERLUDE

Siddhartha's Story

By most accounts, Siddhartha Gautama lived and died about 2,500 years ago. You know him as the Buddha. He was the son of a tribal chief, a member of the ruling class in what is today southern Nepal or northern India. He grew up a prince in his palace, sheltered from the world.

When Siddhartha was a young man, he felt compelled to leave his privileged life in order to see his father's kingdom and to meet the people over whom he would someday rule. Although his father sought to keep him from seeing the pain and adversity of life on his journey, Siddhartha saw an elderly man who was hunched over as he walked. Troubled, Siddhartha asked his charioteer about old age: "Will this evil come to me also?" Upon learning that old age was in fact the fate of all people, Siddhartha became "deeply agitated" and wished to return to the palace.

Later, finding no happiness in his palace, Siddhartha once more journeyed out into his father's kingdom. This time he saw a man afflicted with disease—a swollen belly, his arms hanging loosely at his sides, skin pale and yellow. Once again the young prince asked his charioteer, "Are all beings alike threatened by illness?" Upon learning that all people might contract illnesses like this, Siddhartha became "deeply distressed" and all joy departed from him. He once more asked to return to the palace.

Later, seeing his son despondent from the thought that all human beings will grow old and get sick, Siddhartha's father planned another excursion from the palace, this time with singers and dancers along the road, and he gave clear instructions that no one sick or aged should be seen by his son. Yet on this journey Siddhartha encountered a dead man being carried along by four of his friends. Having never seen death up close, the young prince once again turned to his charioteer and asked if death would eventually come for all. The charioteer replied that death was the fate of all human beings. Siddhartha, according to Buddhism's sacred texts, then "immediately sank down overwhelmed" as he pondered the fate of all human beings. He was suddenly aware of these three somber truths: we will all grow old, get sick, and one day die. *

The nineteenth-century existentialist philosophers have a word for the deeply troubling feelings Siddhartha experienced: angst. *The German word comes from the Greek word* angxo, *which means to strangle as if one can't breathe. It is the Greek root of our word* anxiety.

I recount his story because, like Siddhartha, all of us have moments when we struggle with anxiety about growing old, getting sick, and dying. Perhaps you've known the feeling of anxiety—a feeling like you can't breathe—when contemplating these same concerns. After his encounters with human suffering, Siddhartha devoted himself to finding a way to escape this anxiety, to be free from the fear of the universal fate of human beings. Upon finding release from these fears, he was considered enlightened—the word Buddha *means "the*

How?

---

* For the telling of the Buddha's story I've drawn from Book III of the Buddha-karita of Asvaghosha, which can be read online at http://www .sacred-texts.com/bud/sbe49/sbe4903.htm.

Enlightened One." At points, the teachings of Jesus and the Christian spiritual practices that came later have themes in common with Buddhist thought and practices. But ultimately the Christian faith offers a somewhat different response to the angst of old age, sickness, and death.

None of us is exempt from the deeply troubling feelings surrounding end-of-life concerns. You may not use the word angst *to describe it, but I suspect you know how it feels—that sense of suffering and death closing in, and no escape in sight. In chapters 17, 18, and 19, we'll consider these fears, we'll look at how we find courage and hope in the face of them, and we'll examine the uniquely Christian response to these universal, existential fears.*

17

"I Don't Want to Grow Old!"

Grow old along with me! / The best is yet to be.

—ROBERT BROWNING

Age is an issue of mind over matter. If you don't mind, it doesn't matter.

—ATTRIBUTED TO MARK TWAIN

AS I WRITE THIS CHAPTER, LESTER REED, THE OLDEST member of the church I serve, has just turned 108 years old. He's still amazingly spry, but he did tell me that at his age he never buys green bananas. For years, Lester hardly ever missed a worship service or Sunday school lesson, and he kept a habit of walking over a mile a day. Only recently has he showed signs of slowing down.

What I love about Lester is that he puts age in perspective for me. At fifty-three, I might have fifty-five years left if I were to live as long as Lester. Measured by Lester's life, mine isn't even half over yet. Of course, statistically, it is unlikely that I'll live as long as Lester. Nevertheless, being around him gives me hope.

We'll talk about fear of death in another chapter. But first let's consider how most people feel about growing old. Recently, our thirty-year-old daughter, Danielle, texted LaVon. She was in Kohl's department store and overheard two college girls pointing to a particular shirt that was on display. "I'd never wear something like that!" one of the girls said. "That looks like something a thirty-year-old mom would wear!" Danielle's text read: "I am now the object of young people's derision. So old it's inconceivable!"

AARP produced a video a couple of years ago featuring millennials who were each asked, How old is old? Their answers ranged from the forties to the sixties. They were asked to demonstrate how "old people" would do push-ups or jumping jacks. They acted out with great effort how an "old person" would exercise—hunching their backs in an exaggerated manner and pausing between jumping jacks to take a deep breath. Next, a group of fifty- to seventy-year-olds was brought in to meet each of the millennials. The young people quickly came to redefine what old meant to them as they met these dynamic elders.

SORTING THROUGH FEELINGS ABOUT AGING

LaVon and I were in our late twenties when we found our first gray hairs. Gradually, we began to see crow's-feet around our eyes. But we've discovered that while physically we're aging in step, the emotional hurdles feel different. Turning thirty was no big deal to me—I felt like I had finally become an adult. For LaVon it felt more unsettling—her youth seemed in the past. For me, forty was more difficult—not because I feared growing old, but because I feared becoming irrelevant. I was no longer the young pastor representing a younger generation. I was too old to be hip and yet too young to be wise. I was forty when our first daughter, Danielle, graduated from college and moved away. As I described in chapter 14, becoming an empty nester represented a kind of death—the end of a time of having our kids at home. It hit LaVon in other ways—so much of her life had been spent caring for our kids, and now that season was coming to a close. In our midforties, we struggled with how to do life as empty nesters. We even struggled with our feelings for each other.

With the help of counseling, we tried to sort through our feelings. Thankfully, within a couple of years we had our joy back, and our love for each other deepened. When our kids came home from college, we enjoyed them as adults sharing their lives with us. We were delighted to discover, as other parents have before us, that our IQs seemed to go up as our kids left their teen years behind.

When we turned fifty, we had our first grandchild. People talk about being a grandparent and how amazing it is—yeah, yeah, yeah—but if you are not a grandparent yet, you can't really understand. I can only say that I think I've experienced more joy in my fifties than at any other time in my life. LaVon and I are more in love with each other, with more time to play and more resources than when our children were small. We can buy things for our granddaughter, Stella, and do things with her that we had neither the money nor the time to buy for or do with our kids. I still love my job of twenty-eight years with the church, but now I also enjoy writing, mentoring, traveling, and learning outside of the church as well.

Most of us fear growing old and leaving behind the life stage we're currently in. Few twentysomethings can't wait to turn thirty. Few thirtysomethings are elated to turn forty. And few fortysomethings are thrilled to turn fifty. Yet, what I've found to be true in my life, and in the lives of most of the people I know, is that each stage of life (with a few momentary exceptions) has been better than the one before. And that is precisely what nearly every study on aging shows.

Six years ago, we conducted a survey at Church of the Resurrection of some five thousand people to find out about marital satisfaction. We conducted it again last year. In both surveys we found the same things. Marital satisfaction drops nearly every year during the first twenty years of a marriage. The drop coincides with the stresses and demands of having children and launching one's career (but mostly having children). Then somewhere between years twenty and twenty-five of a marriage, marital happiness levels out and begins to improve. Then it proceeds to climb as dramatically as it dropped, coinciding with kids moving away from home. (Don't get me wrong, the surveys all showed that children were a great source of happiness in marriage, at least prior to their teenage years, but while children were a blessing, they tended to negatively impact the relationship between husband and wife.) The happiest people in our marital survey were not the newlyweds but the people who had been married more than fifty years!

WHEN OLDER = HAPPIER

We fear that the older we get the less happy we'll be, but the evidence suggests just the opposite. In nearly every survey conducted related to aging, as with our marital satisfaction survey, self-reported happiness drops during the twenties, thirties, and forties, reaching a low in the early fifties. It's not that people are unhappy in general; they're just less happy than they were in their early twenties. Why? In the late twenties and beyond, as noted above, people are working hard to launch a career. We're putting in longer hours, we earn less, and we experience more financial stress; young children bring their own demands to the mix. In addition, people in this demographic are likely to move several times.

What happens in the early fifties? Children move out, and grandchildren are born! We usually have more vacation time, higher incomes, and fewer expenses (for example, houses are often paid off). Hopefully, by then we're bringing more wisdom to the desire/self-discipline dynamic we discussed in the previous chapter. All of these factors play some part in the sharp increase in happiness most people experience in their midfifties. The increase continues into the eighties: in many surveys, the happiest people are seventy and older—despite the physical limitations that sometimes come during these decades.* Interestingly, when asked who they think will be happier, both young people and older people believe the younger people must be happier. But when asked to rank their own personal happiness, those over seventy outscore those in their twenties.**

It seems Robert Browning was right when he penned those well-loved lines "Grow old along with me! / The best is yet to be."

Several years ago, I read a remarkable study on happiness and aging conducted at Harvard. The study looked at 268 men over a seventy-five-year period, beginning in 1939. The men would be followed for the rest of their lives. When Professor George

---

* Among the surveys and studies that have found this data to be true is the Gallup-Healthways Well-Being Index. The General Social Survey Final Report, published by NORC at the University of Chicago, recorded that 30.2 percent of those aged eighteen through thirty-four were very happy and 38.5 percent of those over sixty-five reported being very happy. http://norc.org/pdfs/GSS%20Reports/GSS_PsyWellBeing15_final_formatted.pdf.

** One of the latest surveys can be found here: https://www.ons.gov.uk/peoplepopulationandcommunity/wellbeing/articles/measuringnationalwellbeing/atwhatageispersonalwellbeingthehighest.

Vaillant published his findings, the men who were still living were about ninety-five years old. Among Vaillant's conclusions: if you keep your health, "being ninety can be a lot of fun."[*] But his foremost finding was that the key to happiness in old age could be summarized by one word: *love*. This included, for some of his subjects, an awareness of being loved by God, of being loved by others, and a commitment to loving others—the very things Jesus described as the most important commandments.

But there's more we can learn from our seniors. Here are some of the reasons researchers believe older adults are happier than younger adults:

- They have more reasonable expectations.
- They are more appreciative of what they have.
- They have more time to spend with family and friends.
- They tend to have time for hobbies, travel, and other leisure activities.
- They feel less pressure and stress to meet others' expectations.
- They tend to have fewer negative and more positive emotions.
- The breadth of their life experiences leads them to be less overwhelmed by adversity.

These are just a few of the many reasons why people living in the last quarter of their lives are the happiest of all. The most

---

[*] Quoted from a video about the book that detailed the results of the study. The video is found at: http://www.hup.harvard.edu/catalog.php ?isbn-9780674503816. The book is *The Triumph of Experience: The Men of the Harvard Grant Study*, George E. Vaillant (Cambridge: Belknap Press, 2015). See also the TED Talk at https://www.youtube.com /watch?v=WKDsU96EVuk, in which George Vaillant gives a nineteen-minute talk about one man the study collected data on across his entire life.

important thing to notice, if you fear growing older, is simply that everything you thought you knew about growing older is likely wrong. Older adults are doing more, staying more active, and enjoying their lives more than you may have thought, and unless you yourself are in your seventies, they are likely happier than you are right now!

"I THINK I'M LOSING MY MIND"

Among the greatest fears we have about growing older is being stricken with Alzheimer's disease and losing our mind and memories. This is understandable. Many of us, by the time we're in our late forties or early fifties, begin to fear that we may have early-onset Alzheimer's as we struggle to remember names, words, or even facts we've previously known. If I had a dollar for every time a friend of mine told me they worried that they might have Alzheimer's, I'd be rich. But if you're between forty-five and sixty-five, the chance that you have early-onset Alzheimer's is 0.24 percent. In other words, you have a 99.76 percent chance of *not* having Alzheimer's.* Are you forgetting names, where you put your car keys, or other stuff you feel you should know? Welcome to the club. Everyone I know over forty-five talks about forgetting these things and worries they may have Alzheimer's. If they are under sixty-five, the chances are highly unlikely that they do.

---

* My calculations are based on data from the US Census Bureau and the Alzheimer's Association. According to the Census Bureau, there are 81 million Americans between the ages of forty-five and sixty-five. The Alzheimer's Association believes that there are 200,000 Americans between the ages of forty-five and sixty-five who have early-onset Alzheimer's. Divide 200,000 by 81 million and you get a prevalence of 0.24 percent of the population aged forty-five to sixty-five who have Alzheimer's.

Even after sixty-five, the chances of your *not ever having* Alzheimer's are *significantly* higher than that you will one day suffer from the disease. And thankfully, important advances are being made to prevent Alzheimer's, including research at the University of Cambridge that is focused on antibodies custom-designed to prevent the buildup of beta-amyloid proteins in the brain that leads to Alzheimer's-related dementia.[*]

Once more, when we face our fears with faith, examine our assumptions, attack our anxieties with action (which might mean making donations to Alzheimer's research), and release our cares to God, we find it possible to be no longer controlled by our fears.

Another common fear related to aging is that of spending the last years of our lives in a nursing home or care facility. Statistically, only 5 percent of all older adults live in a nursing home or care facility. The chances of needing such a place increase the older we get, so if we focus just on the population aged ninety-five and older, well beyond the average life expectancy of Americans, the number who one day will need a skilled care facility rises to just under 50 percent. The average stay in a nursing home is six months. But some *will* need assisted living facilities. The baby boomers are likely to redefine even this part of aging with new models for skilled care centers.[**]

---

[*] Amirah Al Idrus, "Designer Antibodies Block Alzheimer's Plaque from Forming," FierceBiotech, June 23, 2017, http://www.fiercebiotech.com /research/designer-antibodies-block-alzheimer-s-plaques-from-forming.

[**] David Demko, AgeVenture News Service, www.demko.com, Boca Raton, Florida, at http://nursinghomediaries.com/howmany/.

CLARA AND CELIA BELL ON A MISSION

When I think of those whom I have known who ultimately needed assisted living, I think of Clara. When I visited her care center, I learned that she herself was regularly visiting residents who were no longer able to easily leave their rooms. She saw these visits as her mission and as God's calling for her. I also think of my great-aunt Celia Bell, whose last few months were spent in a care center, but who never stopped seeking to bless and care for those around her. After moving from her own apartment to a small room at the care center, she seemed to me the epitome of someone who was living unafraid, with courage and hope. When I asked her how she lived with such a positive spirit, she said, "There are two things I've learned: be grateful each day, and look for ways to bless other people."

Once more we find that the fears we often carry with us may not match up with the new realities of growing older. It is natural to worry about what will happen as we age, yet we can turn that worry into a gift that motivates us to take care of our bodies or plan for our futures in other ways. It can also lead us to nurture our social relationships, recognizing how important they are both to the quality of our lives and to our longevity.

Studies consistently show—as I noted earlier—that among the contributing factors to happiness and a high quality of life in older adults is their faith and their faith community. The evidence is plain: senior adults with a faith community are simply happier and live longer, and they have more friends who care for one another. I saw this playing out most recently when my eighty-three-year-old mother-in-law broke her hip. She lives on her own, and if you saw her, you'd swear she couldn't be any older than sixty-five. She's sharp, active, and completely independent. Following her hip replacement, she received a steady stream of people visiting her in the hospital and in the rehab center, nearly all of whom were from her church.

But it is not just having a faith community that impacts our quality of life and helps us to face aging with courage and hope. It is the rewards of faith itself. Today's senior adults are the most spiritual and religious of all the generations in America. They are more likely to pray, read scripture, attend worship, give, and serve. At Resurrection, many of our most faithful volunteers are retirees.

When we turn to the scriptures, we find that God has a habit of working in and through older adults. God chose Noah when he was ancient to build the ark and gather the animals on it. Abraham was seventy-five, and Sarah sixty-five, when God called them to head to the Promised Land. Moses was eighty when God called him to return to Egypt to confront Pharaoh and to demand the liberation of the Israelite slaves. Joshua was eighty when he led the Israelites in battle, conquering the Promised Land. King David was still writing his Psalms and making provisions for the building of the temple in Jerusalem well into his seventies. Elijah the prophet was likely a senior citizen when God did his greatest work through him. Without even turning to the many New Testament figures who did noteworthy things in their later years, here are two impressions I have from this quick survey: God often chooses and uses senior adults to do his greatest work, and our greatest adventures often happen when we're past retirement.

REIMAGINING THE LATER YEARS

What if we looked at retirement not as being "put out to pasture" but as being freed up to do more of the things we are passionate about? What if this was a chapter in our lives where we could read, study, and learn more about the things we love, including growing an ever-deepening faith? What if we had the time to serve in ways that used our gifts and abilities, doing things that were meaningful and of interest to us while having a positive impact on those around us and accomplishing God's work in the world?

I think of a retired physician in my church, Myron, who serves as a congregational care minister and volunteers in our student ministry. Now in his seventies, Myron has told me more than once, "I'm having more fun, and finding more meaning and joy in my life, in this decade than I've ever known before." I think of Marty, who, since reaching retirement age, has personally led dozens of small groups studying the Bible and Christian theology. She has mentored over four hundred men and women, helping them to become serious, deeply devout, and critically informed Christians. Each of them in turn has gone on to impact hundreds of other people. I think of Paul, who has devoted hundreds of hours in his retirement to projects benefiting low-income children in Kansas City. I could go on with hundreds of examples of people who found great joy and meaning postretirement in serving God by serving others.

I love the promise of God in Joel 2:28, repeated in Acts 2:17: "I will pour out my spirit upon everyone; your sons and your daughters will prophesy, your old men will dream dreams." If Joel were writing today he would include older women as well. We can infer from this promise that, particularly in our mature years, God will fill us with the Spirit and give us dreams for how we might impact others and the world. It is important for those of us who are not yet "old" to listen to the dreams of our elders, and for elders to pay attention to God's dreams and act upon them.

We can use our imagination to conjure up all the terrible

things that could happen to us as we age. Or we could use that same power to think about the wonderful things we might do in our later years, to imagine the ways God might work through us and the adventures we might have along the way. We can imagine more time with our children and grandchildren, more time with our friends, and more opportunities to learn and grow. And, finally, we can trust that God will stand with us every step along this journey.

Siddhartha famously suffered extreme angst when his innocent assumptions came face-to-face with the realities of age and illness. But our faith in God gives us reasons to move beyond angst. Yes, we are mortal, finite, and likely to suffer. Yes, we'll all grow old. But that's not the whole story. Our lives up to this point have demonstrated again and again that each season brings its own, often unexpected rewards. Whatever our age is today, we can look forward with serenity, even anticipation, to the season that lies ahead. We can live, dream, play, create, and worship with confidence that the "best is yet to be."

18

Anxiety, Worry, and Physical Illness

Anxiety is a thin stream of fear trickling through the mind. If encouraged, it cuts a channel into which all other thoughts are drained.

—ARTHUR SOMERS ROCHE

Luckily, most of your anxiety is self-created and can be uncreated.

—ALBERT ELLIS

MY CAR IS CONSTANTLY TALKING TO ME, AND IF YOU'VE got a newer car, I'm guessing yours talks to you too. A decade or two ago this would have been unimaginable, but today my car is constantly giving me feedback. Its multiple sensors and myriad computers greet me when I get in and quickly run through a check of its eight computer systems. Yesterday my car greeted me with the notice that my left rear tire needed more air. Today, as I was driving my wife's Ford Fusion, the steering wheel began to vibrate, a bell chimed, and the message center on my dash indicated *the car* thought I was driving erratically and suggested I stop for a cup of coffee! (Yes, this really happened. LaVon's car monitors the lines on the road and thought I had swerved near them one too many times.)

I believe that the marvels of a living human being will always surpass the marvels of technology, but I see an analogy here that can help us think about anxiety and illness. We've learned that, like a modern car, the body's system of sensors constantly scans our surroundings to alert us to possible dangers. Our senses and intuition stream information to the brain—specifically to the amygdala—about what's happening in and around us. Scripture says that we are "fearfully and wonderfully made," and this is clearly evident in the body's ability to send a message if something is wrong.

One night several years ago, I felt a sharp pain in my abdomen. LaVon was out of town, and I lay in bed waiting for the pain to go away. Eventually I got up and took something I hoped would ease what I thought was an upset stomach. But the pain would not subside. The longer I lay there, the more I began to worry that something more serious might be up. Finally, at 3 a.m., I drove myself to the emergency room where, a couple of hours later, I learned my gallbladder was unhappy and the doctors said it needed to go.

And this is precisely how the body is supposed to work—I didn't know the source of my discomfort and pain, but the sensations became uncomfortable enough that I sought help. Yet as wonderful as our bodies are, our sensory system can sometimes send false alarms. It may want us to spring into action against a threat that's not there or is quite minor. Regardless, we can feel fear, worry, or anxiety. The current of anxiety can grow from "a thin stream of fear" to the point where "it cuts a channel into which all other thoughts are drained," completely overwhelming ordinarily calm people.

Over the last thirty years I've walked with hundreds of people as they battled cancer, serious heart conditions, ALS, and a host of other frightening medical diagnoses. In this chapter,

I'll share what I've learned from them. I've also walked with people who battled panic and anxiety related to their health, experiencing physical symptoms for which doctors could find no medical cause. Panic, anxiety, and hypochondria are all conditions related either to hypersensitivity in the body's sensors or to false alarms (false events appearing real, as we described them earlier). This issue struck particularly close to home twenty years ago, when my wife was in and out of the hospital with symptoms for which there was no clear diagnosis other than the feeling itself—in her case, it was anxiety. We'll share a bit of her story later in this chapter.

FALSE ALARMS AND MIXED MESSAGES

It is true that some people have a greater sensitivity to what's happening in their body than the general population. For example, they can sense changes in their blood pressure, heart rate or rhythm, and breathing that the average person might miss. When they become aware of changes or irregularities in their body, they may struggle more to decipher if these are serious issues or "normal abnormalities."

Adding to the confusion is that the autonomic nervous system (ANS) transmits signals both to and from the brain. The brain might see a possible threat and send signals through the ANS aimed at preparing the body for some as yet unclear threat. We learned in chapter 2 that the body's fight-or-flight mechanism prepares it for action in the face of danger—familiar physical reactions can include a rapid heartbeat or palpitations, shallow, rapid breathing (hyperventilation), and muscles tensing up. Our hands might feel clammy, we might perspire, or we might begin to feel weak or to shake. The brain triggers these responses in the face of not only real threats but also imagined threats, or when we've misinterpreted data from our senses or perceptions at the subconscious level.

In the absence of any clear medical condition or some other real danger, our brain struggles to know, *Is my heart racing because something is wrong with my heart? Does my struggle to breathe point to a problem with my lungs? Is it possible something is wrong with my brain—a brain tumor, perhaps? Could there be some other real danger I simply can't see? Or are these symptoms triggered by a false event appearing real?* We can be left with a chicken-and-egg scenario—unable to figure out which came first, the feeling of threat or the threat itself.

Most people who struggle with health-related anxiety or panic find it difficult, at first, to accept that anxiety is a real issue. The symptoms, after all, are very real. They usually are not aware, at a conscious level, that there is anything about which they could possibly be anxious. When a doctor, a friend, a spouse, or a counselor suggests anxiety as the underlying problem, the sufferers can easily feel that they, or their experiences, are not being taken seriously. They might feel angry, frustrated, or hurt by the suggestion that anxiety is the cause, not the result, of their symptoms. They might respond, "I am not anxious. I've got nothing to be anxious about. Things are going well in my life. I've just got these real symptoms. Stop suggesting it's anxiety!"

But sometimes it *is* anxiety. Our brain's early warning and threat detection system is constantly learning about new threats to our health. Our brain stores this new information alongside all the other potential dangers it has cataloged from our earliest memories. Advertising and the Internet have played a key role in exacerbating the problem, leaving us confused and wondering about a host of possible risks to our health and well-being.

Let's consider some of the things that might play a role in

increasing our conscious or subconscious concerns about our health. In the decades since May 19, 1983, when the first prescription drug ad ran on television, commercials for over-the-counter and prescribed drugs have become ubiquitous. These ads encourage us to self-diagnose medical problems we might otherwise never have known existed. The Nielsen ratings organization estimates that eighty commercials for medications run on TV *every hour.*[*] Drug companies spend $5.2 billion annually in direct marketing to consumers.[**] Pharmaceutical advertising raises the specter of illnesses to consumers.

And then there's the Internet. What a gift, and what a curse, that we have access to more health information than at any time in human history. We feel something—a heart flutter, a pain in the side, a bump, a spasm, or anything else that just doesn't seem right—go online, and diagnose ourselves by Googling it. A quick Internet search can provide lots of fuel for our subconscious self to perceive danger. There are 345 distinct medical conditions listed at MedicineNet.com, and that's just those that begin with the letter *A*! We wonder if we have one or another of these illnesses that seem to coincide with the particular symptoms we are feeling. A meme you may have seen online captures these ruminations: "Google—Creating Hypochondriacs Since 1998."

---

[*] Alix Spiegel, "Selling Sickness: How Drug Ads Changed Health Care," NPR, *Morning Edition*, October 13, 2009, http://www.npr.org/templates /story/story.php?storyId=113675737.

[**] Aimee Picchi, "Drug Ads: $5.2 Billion Annually—and Rising," CBSNews .com (*Moneywatch*), March 11, 2016.

WHAT ARE THE CHANCES?

Daniel Gardner, in *The Science of Fear,* argues that the way in which data is presented has the power either to raise our fears or to calm them. Here's one example from the disease Americans fear the most: cancer. The American Cancer Society notes that men have a one in four chance of dying of cancer; for women, the odds are one in five. One in four sounds like pretty high odds and plays to the fears we already have about cancer. But let's look more carefully at the data and present it in a slightly different way.

First—and this is minor—the percentage of men who will die of cancer is actually 22 percent, which is a bit lower than 25 percent. But what happens if we take out those who are smokers? For men, the number drops to 15 percent. In other words, the chance that a nonsmoking man will die of cancer is not 1 in 4, but 1 in 6.5. That's not quite as scary, but it still sounds like a large number. What if we said that of every one hundred nonsmokers, only fifteen will die of cancer? Or, said another way, that of every one hundred men who don't smoke, eighty-five will *not* die of cancer? Let's put it as a percentage: nonsmoking men have an 85 percent chance of *not* dying of cancer. When we say it this way, my odds as a nonsmoking man of *not* dying of cancer are actually pretty good. Consider this analogy: if a meteorologist tells you that there's an 85 percent chance of sunshine tomorrow, will you cancel your picnic or ball game? Nonsmoking ladies, your odds of *not* dying of cancer are even better.

Cancer is also largely a disease that afflicts older adults. Yet many young people fear it. The odds of dying of cancer before your sixtieth birthday are just 0.5 percent (meaning that you have a 99.5 percent chance of *not* dying of cancer in your thirties, forties, and fifties). As we've seen throughout this book, we can worry about a lot of things that will never happen to us, including cancer.

For our present purposes, I'd offer this definition of worry (and, by extension, *anxiety* and other words we use to describe this unhappy state): <u>Worry is imagining a negative future that may never (and likely will never) happen.</u> Jesus addresses this in the Sermon on the Mount: "Who among you by worrying can add a single moment to your life?" (Matthew 6:27). He goes on to say, "Therefore, stop worrying about tomorrow, because tomorrow will worry about itself" (Matthew 6:34). In other words, don't take the things that may or may not happen in the future and drag them into your present.

As I write these words, I'm watching the music video of Bobby McFerrin's 1988 hit song "Don't Worry, Be Happy." Wouldn't it be great if it was as simple as that? But it's not, or you wouldn't be reading this book. As we've seen, we all carry with us a measure of worry, fear, or anxiety. And while some fear is good and healthy, fear in the form of worry or anxiety brings recurring pain to many people. This is particularly so for the forty million Americans who suffer from anxiety disorders.*

---

* "Anxiety and Physical Illness," Harvard Health Publications, July 2008 (updated June 6, 2017), http://www.health.harvard.edu/staying-healthy /anxiety_and_physical_illness.

CHASING ANXIETY DISORDER OUT INTO THE LIGHT

My wife is one of those people. It was the fall of 1996. We were at a clergy gathering when LaVon began to feel ill. Her heart began to race, her palms grew sweaty, and she felt that there was something wrong happening in her body. We quickly left the party and ended up driving to the emergency room of a nearby hospital. The ER doctor checked out her heart and ran a series of tests. He found nothing that night, but asked her to visit an internist, which she did. He ran a battery of tests without finding anything at first. Over the next few months we were in and out of the emergency room with similar symptoms. As terrifying as the symptoms were, even worse was the doctors' inability to diagnose what was wrong in an otherwise healthy thirty-three-year-old woman.

Several months later, a possible diagnosis surfaced—small blood clots in the lungs. We felt tremendous relief to finally know *something*. The doctors began to treat the blood clots. At the same time, LaVon started to explore the possibility that some of what she was enduring might be related to anxiety. As she began to read about how others experienced anxiety and panic, she recognized a similarity between their experiences and her own and realized that for those who suffer with anxiety or panic, the symptoms are very real and physiological, but they can be triggered by the body's early warning system misfiring—giving the brain false alarms—rather than any actual imminent danger. I asked her if she would be willing to share some of her story for this book, and here it is, in her words.

I have always been a bit of a worrier—I come by it naturally from my family of origin—but it became a debilitating factor in my life not long after my thirty-third birthday. I'm not sure what the exact trigger was, but I became obsessed with thinking there was something physically wrong with me. The obsession increased the general physical feelings I was having: racing heart, tingly hands, shortness of breath, depression, and fatigue. After rushing to the hospital three times thinking I was near death (panic attacks), a myriad of medical tests to try to figure out what was physically wrong, and months of retreating from myself and the world around me, I finally came to the realization that what I was dealing with was anxiety.

I knew I had to do something to change my way of thinking and reacting to the world around me. I had gotten to such a dark place in my head that I was not able to leave the house alone, drive a car, work, or function as a wife and mother to our two young children. It was not easy to identify the problem as anxiety, to accept it and admit it to myself and others, and an even harder path to overcome it.

I wish I could say that I came through that dark period of my life and never had to deal with the struggle again, but that would not be the case. I liken anxiety and fear to the weeds that I constantly battle in the flower beds at my house. I work hard to clean my beds of weeds, only to be taken by surprise the next day, when a weed that has been lying dormant pops its ugly head above the surface. The same is true with anxiety and fear. The moment I think I have overcome my fear, I am confronted with a different situation that brings it all back again.

As I was journeying out of my very dark place that I was trapped in, into a place of light and life, there were certain things that I did that I found to help. Even now

*I depend on these techniques to help me in times when I
become anxious and fearful.*

*I admitted my fears to my husband, who heard me re-
iterate the same fear daily, sometimes hourly. He didn't
judge me, but helped me talk through my struggles and
reassured me. But I also needed to talk to people who
had struggled with anxiety themselves, and had found a
way to not be controlled by it. This gave me encouragement and hope. And I found it extremely helpful to find a
counselor who specialized in anxiety disorders. A trained
counselor can give you tools and exercises you need to
restructure your fearful thinking into healthier ways of
living and thinking.*

*For a while I was seeing both a psychologist and a psy-
chiatrist. The psychiatrist put me on medication. Many
people who struggle with anxiety are also afraid of medicine, making it hard to trust that medication is safe and
the right thing to do. I found, especially in the beginning
of my journey, that I needed the medication to quiet down
my mind long enough to allow me to do the cognitive
work that was essential to change my way of thinking.*

*Anxiety sufferers become so trapped within their own
selves that it is vital that they force themselves to go out
into the world and find ways to help others. The natural
tendency is to turn inward, protecting the self, but continuing to focus on what's wrong and how scared you are
does nothing but cause the cycle of fear and anxiety to
continue to increase and be fed. As you force yourself to
look for ways to help others, it can break the cycle and it
becomes no longer just about you.*

*I sought out activities in my life that brought me peace,
such as exercise, playing the piano, taking my dog for*

walks, and daily time in Bible study. It was also helpful to find people I trusted who truly understood what I was going through. My husband was great at listening and encouraging, but he had not personally struggled with anxiety. Talking to a friend who had the same struggle but was now living in a place of peace was such a huge help.

Ultimately, it was my faith that gave me the only peace that lasts. It is a daily practice to trust that God is the One who holds my life. As much as I try to control the situation around me, I can't. It's exhausting to try. Time and time again I have to let go and trust that if I live or die, either way, my life is in his hands and in knowing that there is peace.

Watching LaVon's battle with anxiety was part of what inspired me to write this book. While most of us will experience intense anxiety and even bouts of panic at times, those who struggle with anxiety disorders and chronic panic attacks know what it's like when fear controls you. But over a two-year period, I watched LaVon move from panic and anxiety controlling her life to living with courage and hope. Although she did not completely eliminate anxiety, she controls it most of the time now, rather than letting it control her.

YOU ARE NOT LESSER OR WEAKER

Among the things that helped LaVon in her battle with anxiety was, as we've learned throughout the book, facing her fears with faith, examining her anxieties in light of the facts, attacking her anxieties with action, and releasing her cares and worries to God. She also had the help of anti-anxiety medications, a caring counselor, and friends and family. Today you would never guess that she struggled with anxiety, and still does at times. She is the strong, bold, courageous woman I knew before the panic set in. And that's part of the message I think is important for those who struggle with the same disorders. You may be among those who suffer with a greater than ordinary degree of worry about your health. (Going back to the car analogy, you may simply be wired with more sensitive sensors than others.) That doesn't mean you are somehow lesser or weaker—physically, morally, or spiritually. You may simply be more vulnerable to fear in the guise of anxiety, panic, and worry. Nevertheless, you don't have to give anxiety control over your life. You can live with courage. You can overcome this. There is hope for you!*

That brings me back to the question of fear as it relates to our health. Whatever level of sensitivity to fear we live with, often the older we get the more fearful we become. What's perplexing is that by all outward measures, we have less to fear or worry about than at any time in the history of the human race. We're living longer than any previous generation. We've defeated most of the terrible childhood diseases of the past. And medical researchers are making amazing advances.

Yet, despite all of this, we still struggle with fear. Daniel

---

* I've tried to cover a wide array of fears, anxieties, and worries in this book. I trust it will prove helpful, encouraging, and hopeful. If you struggle with debilitating anxiety, this book will likely be just one among many that you have read or will read. If you want to go deeper, take a look at Rena Goldman's suggestions in "13 Books That Shine a Light on Anxiety," Healthline.com, July 11, 2017. Among the books LaVon found very helpful is Lucinda Bassett's *From Panic to Power*. Our congregational care department recommends *How to Control Your Anxiety Before It Controls You* by Albert Ellis.

Gardner writes: "We are the healthiest, wealthiest, and longest-lived people in history. And we are increasingly afraid. This is one of the great paradoxes of our time."

WHAT WE GAIN FROM MINDFULNESS

So, how do we refrain from worrying about and stressing over what might happen? Buddhists, Christians, and therapists of all kinds agree that part of the solution is something called *mindfulness*. I sat down with James Cochran, the director of our counseling ministry at Church of the Resurrection, who noted the reasons why mindfulness matters:

> *So much of the anxiety we experience is a product of bringing the future into the present. . . . We think about what could happen, what might happen. It is like cramming all of this future experience into the present. We don't allow ourselves any time in the present to feel freedom or joy or to engage meaningfully in our relationships. As a consequence of that we feel anxious, we feel worried, we feel fear. The formal practice of mindfulness is geared toward allowing us to push away the depression or sadness from ruminating on the past, and the worry, fear, and anxiety from thinking about the future, and instead allows us to be engaged in the present moment.*

James, like many counselors, often encourages using breathing techniques as a tool to help us live in the present. When we get anxious, our breathing becomes shallow and our oxygen intake decreases, which increases our feelings of discomfort or fear about some unpleasant future. Slowing down to breathe not only improves our oxygen intake, but it helps us to become mindful of the present moment. James recommends what is often called four-sided breathing, or square breathing. You can stop at any point in the day and try this little exercise:

- Breathe in slowly counting to four.
- Hold your breath to the count of four.
- Exhale slowly, counting to four as you exhale.
- Hold the exhale, lungs empty, to the count of four.

Doing this slows down your breathing. It relaxes your body and focuses your mind on the present moment rather than on a fearful future. It is easy to add meditation and prayer to this practice. You can give thanks or recite encouraging scriptures, like God's promise we encountered in an earlier chapter: "Do not be afraid, for I am with you."

Here, technology can become an ally of our intentions. People I know use smartphones or Outlook calendars to prompt a contemplative practice during the day. My Apple watch comes built in with a program to encourage this kind of breathing. I can set it to invite me to stop and practice this form of breathing as often as I wish. When it vibrates on my wrist, I stop to breathe, and as I do, I offer a "breath prayer"—a short one-sentence prayer like "I belong to you, O Lord," or "Thank you, Lord, for the blessings of today." I may pray, "You are my shepherd" or "I love you, O Lord."

Part of what I like about mindfulness and living in the present is that when I do this—when I am really paying attention to what is going on around me—I take my eyes off of myself, I stop thinking about my illness or troubles or concerns, and instead I find myself thinking of God and others.

FACING ILLNESS WITH COURAGE AND HOPE

We've been speaking primarily about health-related anxiety where the perceived health condition is the result of hypersensitivity, false alarms, or anxiety itself. But what about addressing the fear we feel when we do have a serious illness? As a pastor I've made hundreds of hospital calls and sat in the homes of hundreds of people facing frightening diagnoses. I've prayed with and cared for people battling cancer. Most survived; for others, their situations were terminal. I've been to visit the dying at our area hospice palliative care center. I've cared for a half-dozen people who faced lengthy battles with ALS. I've been moved and inspired by so many of these people, learning from them how they faced illness with courage and hope. I'd like to share a few of their stories with you.

One woman in the congregation suffered from a debilitating terminal illness that made it difficult for her to speak and move, but left her fully conscious of what was happening around her. She knew fear in the face of her illness and progressively worsening condition. But two things seemed to give her hope and courage: a trust that her life belonged to God, was a gift from God, and that, ultimately, she was safe in his arms (we'll consider this idea more in the next chapter), and her intentional decision to concentrate on serving others and focusing on their needs rather than on her illness.

On one of my visits to the hospital to see her, her husband stood on one side of the bed, and I stood on the other as we held her hands. Her husband told me that though she had very limited mobility and could barely communicate anymore (I believe he was the only who could understand her), she was focusing on praying for others. She had noticed the life-flight helicopters landing at the hospital. She communicated to her husband that whenever she heard a helicopter landing, she would begin praying. In silence, in the thoughts of her heart, she prayed for the patient in the helicopter, the doctors, the nurses, and the pilots. The act of praying for and blessing the people who crossed her path brought meaning and purpose to her final weeks.

Scott Cart and his family have taught me about the importance of facing frightening illness by living one day at a time and giving thanks for each day. In 2005, at age thirty-four, he was diagnosed with amyotrophic lateral sclerosis, or ALS, often referred to as Lou Gehrig's disease. The doctors told him that he likely had three to five years to live. Scott has lived well beyond the expectations of his doctors. Though his speech is impeded, and he doesn't move his arms as he once did, he and his family are in worship most weekends. He is still very active in his daughters' lives, and there is a joy I see in him and in his family that is all the more beautiful because of his illness.

Not long ago, I visited Scott and his wife, Sheila, and their two teenage daughters, Kaylee and Marissa, in their home. I wanted to find out more about how he and his family face ALS, one of the most frightening of illnesses. Scott told me that when he was first diagnosed, he felt his whole world was crumbling. He was angry and afraid, and he wanted to know "Why me?" But soon, he said, "I realized that wasn't going to help anything. I could spend all my time focused on the disease and my disappointment, or I could choose to focus on the things I loved, on the good things—the blessings." Sheila noted, "We lived with the motto 'Live for the now,' not putting things off because we didn't know how much time we had."

Scott told me that he decided to focus on his family and to trust God. They take vacations, have family time, and laugh a lot. Scott noted, "I'm just grateful for where I am at this point. I pray each day, but my prayers are less about asking for things and more about thanking God for every good thing in my life." And Scott and Sheila and their kids have gotten involved in the fight to raise money for ALS research. The Carts don't believe God gave Scott ALS. Though they would gladly accept a miracle, they also know that this is not how God typically works; instead, he works through medical researchers and doctors, and for that reason the family supports the mission of the ALS Association. But Scott does believe that life is a gift from God, and in giving thanks he finds peace.

As I left Scott and Sheila's home, I was inspired, and I was reminded of the words of Psalm 146:2, "I will praise the Lord with all my life; I will sing praises to my God as long as I live." That's how Scott and his family live their lives.

I have hundreds of other examples, but I'll end with just one more. As I finished writing about Scott and his family, the phone rang. It was Allen, returning my call. I'd reached out to him to see if he might have anything to say about overcoming fear in the face of a serious illness. Allen is thirty-eight and waging a battle with leukemia that he may not win. He's hoping to be accepted for one final experimental trial that appears to be his last hope for medical treatment.

ALLEN'S STORY

Allen began his career as a lawyer and had a bright future ahead of him. That's when I first met him and eventually became his pastor. Several years later, he began to feel a call to ordained ministry. His wife was supportive and Allen went to seminary and eventually was ordained as a United Methodist pastor. He was serving a large congregation in a northern suburb of Kansas City when he received his diagnosis.

Allen noted the three types of fear he's dealt with: the fear of death, the fear of pain, and the fear for his family. He was afraid not only about the emotional impact his death would have on his parents and his wife, Ashley, but also about mundane things like how his wife would deal with their finances after his death. "There are so many things I can't control," he said, "but I have been able to work on an estate plan and sought to make things as easy as possible on Ashley in the event of my death." His call several months ago asking me to preach his funeral was an example of his making preparations so that Ashley wouldn't have to. We've discussed this strategy throughout the book as attacking your anxieties with actions. He spoke with his doctors about his fear of pain; they assured him that they could effectively control it with the pain meds currently available. That was reassuring to him.

But when it came to the fear of death, he told me that he simply did not feel afraid. "Years ago I came to accept that we are mortal creatures, that we are going to die," he said. "We have no guarantees, Adam, as to how long we'll live. Being human means we're going to die. My faith has played a huge part in eliminating the fear of sickness and death. As you've taught us, and Frederick Buechner before you, because of Jesus Christ, the worst thing is not the last thing. My faith in him changed everything on this front. Because of his death and resurrection, I am not afraid to die." This sounded an awfully lot like facing our fears with faith, and releasing our worries and cares to God.

He then told me, "I may not be serving as the pastor of the Liberty United Methodist Church anymore. But every day, even in the midst of this illness, there is always an opportunity to love and bless others. My mission field has often been Units 40 and 41 at the University of Kansas Medical Center, where I have hoped to bless and encourage the doctors and nurses, as well as my family and friends." In this Allen reminded me of the Apostle Paul, who, writing from a prison cell in Rome, told the Christians living in Philippi that he was grateful for his imprisonment, because it had allowed him to share the Gospel with the prison guard (Philippians 1:12–13).

Finally, Allen told me that among the things that had brought him peace were prayer and meditation. "I have not set aside time to pray—*my entire existence* is becoming an ongoing prayer, a conversation and togetherness with God that has resulted in a peace that continues to grow."

FINDING PEACE, RELEASING WORRY

Here's the lesson I want you to take away from those three examples of people facing serious illness: You likely will have some fear if you are ever diagnosed with a serious illness, but that fear doesn't need to control you. It is possible to face even the most frightening of illnesses with courage and hope. Those three persons each came to a place where they accepted their mortality, recognizing that none of us knows how long we'll live. They gratefully accepted each day as a gift, and sought to live it as fully as they could. They continued to look for ways to help, encourage, or bless others, thereby finding meaning and purpose in their illness. They controlled what they could control, and found it helpful to take action where possible. And, ultimately, they found peace in releasing their worry, fear, anxiety, and very lives to God.

Earlier, we noted the words of Jesus: "Who among you by worrying can add a single moment to your life? . . . Therefore, stop worrying about tomorrow, because tomorrow will worry about itself" (Matthew 6:27, 34). The message is clear: Worry and anxiety accomplish *nothing,* but we can do *something.* We can choose a better way.

The Buddha's charioteer was right—we all get sick sometimes. Yet your body is amazing in its capacity to heal itself. And when it can't, we have doctors to care for us. When you feel something is wrong in your body, get it checked out. But don't allow your imagination and your amygdala to spend too much time envisioning all the horrible things that might be wrong. Instead,

Face your fears with faith.
Examine your assumptions in light of the facts (your
    doctor may need to help you here).
Attack your anxieties with action.
Release your cares to God.

That's what I so often see in people who approach their health-related anxieties with courage and hope.

19

"I'm Not Ready to Die"

I'm not afraid of death; I just don't want to be there when it happens.

—WOODY ALLEN

Though I walk through the valley of the shadow of death, I will fear no evil; for Thou art with me.

—PSALM 23:4

DEATH LOOMS LARGE IN THE LIFE OF A PASTOR. WHILE I was writing this chapter, I received a phone call from a young man whose father had died. Through tears, he told me he couldn't bear the thought that he'd never see his father's face again, or hear his voice. His tears and sorrow overwhelmed me too. Three days earlier, I was with the parents and grandparents of a young man who had died in an accident. How could a person with so much promise, and so many good years ahead to realize his dreams, be suddenly gone? Three days before that, I sat with a man in his sixties whose death was imminent. He'd lived a full life, but what came next? He'd not been particularly religious as an adult, but now he wanted to talk to a pastor about death and the afterlife. Death is a regular part of my ministry as a pastor because death is a regular part of life.

We don't know *when* our death will happen, or *how* it will happen, but we do know *that* it will happen. Death is our common end as human beings. As we ponder our own passing, it is natural to feel some worry, fear, or anxiety—it means our brain's early warning system is doing its job. Fear is our body's way of warning us of an impending threat. I'm sure you've noticed that people tend to process this fear in very different ways. Some stay on a prolonged search for pleasure or distraction (remember Solomon's story in chapter 15?). Some try not to think about death—a strategy of denial—which works pretty well until a friend or close family member dies, or we face the real possibility of our own imminent death. For many, anxiety about death has less to do with the act of dying itself, and more to do with anticipating the grief of no longer being with loved ones. Yet whether we're anxious about dying, or simply afraid of being separated from our loved ones, we must come to terms with death.

These strategies of delaying the inevitable reckoning only get more complicated as technology and improved standards of living extend life expectancies virtually around the globe. According to the Social Security Administration's period life table, a boy born just fifty years ago could expect to live to the age of sixty-six, a girl to seventy-five. A boy born this year is expected to live to age seventy-six, a girl to eighty-one. Yet that is not the end of the story. Every year you live, your life expectancy increases. Since I've successfully made it to fifty-three, as of the writing of this book, according to the Social Security Administration's actuarial table, I can expect to live to age eighty; and if I make it to eighty, I can expect to live to be eighty-eight; and once I hit eighty-eight, it's likely I'll make it to ninety-two. The game continues until 120, at which point the

table stops.* But no actuarial table can change the most important reality: we're all going to die. I have preached at funerals
for many people who died unexpectedly, and it is clear to me
that none of us knows when we leave the house in the morning
whether we're going to make it home that night.

The questions for us in this chapter are: How do we live life
well, knowing that death is our common end and could come at
any time? How can we face each day without fear, but instead
with courage and hope?

THE CHRISTIAN VIEW OF DEATH AND WHAT COMES AFTER

Atheists, agnostics, philosophers, and the major world religions
offer various answers to the question of what happens to us
when we die. For some the answer is simple acceptance of the
permanence of death; for others there is the promise of a form
of afterlife; some believe in reincarnation. I leave it to you to
explore their answers. Here, I'd like to take a deeper look at
the answers that the Christian faith brings to questions about
death, dying, and the afterlife. For many, myself included, these
answers—especially as expressed in the Christian concept of
resurrection—provide peace, comfort, courage, and hope in
the face of our mortality.

Let's start with the basics: Christians believe that there is
more to human beings than our material body. The English
New Testament, for example, translates various Greek words

---

* "Life Expectancy in the USA, 1900–98," http://u.demog.berkeley.edu
/~andrew/1918/figure2.html; Felicitie C. Bell and Michael L. Miller, Life
Tables for the United States Social Security Area 1900–2100," Social Security Administration, August 2005, https://www.ssa.gov/oact/NOTES
/pdf_studies/study120.pdf.

used by New Testament authors to describe the human being variously as spirit, mind, soul, heart, as well as body.

When it comes to our physical bodies, Saint Paul describes them in 2 Corinthians 4:7 as "clay pots." For his audience, this was a vivid metaphor. Earthen jars were easily made from clay and water and were used by everyone for storing food and valuables. But they wouldn't last forever. When they broke or wore out, they were tossed aside. If you've ever visited archaeological sites in Israel or elsewhere in the Middle East, you might have seen clay fragments scattered around.

Paul makes this comparison not to disparage our bodies, but to remind us that they aren't intended to last forever. As he notes in 2 Corinthians 5:1, "We know that if the earthly tent we live in is destroyed, we have a building from God, a house not made with hands, eternal in the heavens." The essential self that Paul speaks of here will, by the grace of God, continue to live on after the "earthly tent" of our physical body no longer exists.

I love how Paul describes death not as a horrible end that must be feared but instead as an essential process by which "what is mortal may be swallowed up by life" (2 Corinthians 5:4*b*). Paul describes that essential life that is us, that transcends death, as a "treasure" (2 Corinthians 4:7) and as "our inner nature" (2 Corinthians 4:16).

I've sat with many people whose minds were sharp but whose bodies were obviously failing. One Bible passage that so often resonates with Christians at such times, capturing the spirit of hope and courage that animates them, are these words, also from 2 Corinthians: "So we do not lose heart. Even though our outer nature is wasting away, our inner nature is being renewed day by day. For this slight momentary affliction is preparing us for an eternal weight of glory beyond all measure, because we look not at what can be seen but at what cannot be seen; for what can be seen is temporary, but what cannot be seen is eternal" (2 Corinthians 4:16–18).

It is remarkable to be in the company of people of deep faith, who, like the apostle, are persuaded that death is not the end of their story. They may still feel the physical and emotional fear that originates in the amygdala, but they are not controlled by that fear. They are, as I've used the word throughout this book, *unafraid*.

WHAT DOES "WE WILL ALL BE CHANGED" MEAN?

How is it that our essential self continues when the brain, which seems to serve as our hard drive and central processing unit, no longer lives? And how does such a transfer from our physical body to whatever spiritual body God has prepared for us actually occur?

I use an iPhone. My phone was several years (and three models) old and starting to run a bit slower, the charge wasn't lasting as long, the memory was full, and the phone seemed to need to restart from time to time. So I purchased a new one. The new phone came with upgraded features. It was faster and had more memory and new capabilities. I opened the box, powered it up, and logged in using my e-mail and password from my old phone, and voilà: my pictures, songs, videos, e-mail, texts, apps, and files—all of my memories—on my previous phone showed up on my new phone, having been stored in "the cloud." As I watched my new phone come alive, with all my old data on it, it struck me that this process was analogous to what Christians believe happens in our death and resurrection: everything that makes us us—our thoughts, memories, personality—will continue to exist, albeit in an imperishable (upgraded!) body, a spiritual body, with God.

As I was working on this chapter, a story ran on National Public Radio about a team of physicists from China who had "successfully 'teleported' information on a photon from earth to space, spanning a distance of more than 300 miles."* I admit I don't fully understand quantum physics, but as I heard this story I wondered if it might well point to the "how" of Paul's words that "we will all be changed" as we leave this earthly body behind and receive a new spiritual body. The New Testament teaches that our new "spiritual body" will not be subject to illness or death. Paul writes, "When the rotting body has been clothed in what can't decay, and the dying body has been clothed in what can't die, then this statement from scripture about history's ultimate destination will come to be: Death has been swallowed up by a victory" (1 Corinthians 15:54).

Paul sees death not as a defeat but as a victory. I love how Natalie Sleeth captured it in her 1985 hymn, written as she was pondering the death of a friend:

> *In our end is our beginning; in our time, infinity;*
> *In our doubt there is believing; in our life, eternity,*
> *In our death, a resurrection; at the last, a victory,*
> *Unrevealed until its season, something God alone*
>   *can see.*

Upgrading phones, storing data in the cloud, and "teleporting" photons in quantum physics are all things that once would

---

* Tori Whitley, "Beam Me Up, Scotty . . . Sort Of. Chinese Scientists 'Teleport' Photon to Space," NPR, *Morning Edition*, July 14, 2017, http://www.npr.org/2017/07/14/537174817/scientists-teleport-a-photon-into-space.

have seemed impossible, incomprehensible, or unimaginable to the brightest of people. But today we know they are possible and, in the case of smartphones and the cloud, commonplace. Similarly, the Christian idea that you are more than the electrical impulses that flash across your brain, and that you may survive death, receiving an imperishable body, seems absurd to some but quite believable to me, and it seems so because of what Jesus said about death, and because of the Gospel accounts of his resurrection.

JESUS SAID ANOTHER REALM EXISTS

Let's consider what Jesus said about death. Throughout Matthew, Mark, and Luke, Jesus speaks of eternal life, yet it's a relatively minor theme. In these Gospels, Jesus's primary concern is teaching us how to live now so that God's kingdom might come "on earth as it is in heaven." Still, Jesus clearly teaches that another realm exists in which God's will *is* done, and where those who have gone before us reside with God.

It is in John's Gospel that we find Jesus speaking more fully about the afterlife, and as something we begin to experience on earth, not only after death.

In John 11, Jesus receives word that his friend Lazarus has died, leaving behind his sisters, Martha and Mary. Jesus returns to Lazarus's village of Bethany, just outside of Jerusalem. As Jesus approaches Bethany, Lazarus's sister Martha runs out to greet him. Grieving, she says, "Lord, if you had been here, my brother wouldn't have died." In response Jesus says to her, "I am the resurrection and the life. Whoever believes in me will live, even though they die. Everyone who lives and believes in me will never die" (John 11:21, 25–26). If you've attended a

Christian funeral, you've probably heard these powerful words spoken at the beginning of the service.

On the night before his death, Jesus spoke to his disciples about what was about to occur. Seeing their confused and troubled expressions, he then said, "Don't be troubled. Trust in God. Trust also in me. My Father's house has room to spare. If that weren't the case, would I have told you that I'm going to prepare a place for you? When I go to prepare a place for you, I will return and take you to be with me so that where I am you will be too" (John 14:1–4). I love the imagery of heaven being God's house and having "room to spare" (the King James Version of 1611 translates the first part of this passage as "In my Father's house are many mansions"). But I also love the imagery of Jesus saying "*I* will return and take you to be with me" (emphasis added). When caring for those who are dying, I've found this thought comforting. Jesus doesn't say he'll send his angels at the hour of our death; he says that he himself will come for us when we die.

Of course, this promise would be meaningless except that thirty-six hours after Jesus died the tomb where his body had been laid was discovered to be empty, and suddenly he began appearing to his disciples. Paul gives us the earliest written accounts of the resurrection (the Gospels were written twenty to forty years after Paul wrote his first letter), noting that at one point over five hundred people saw the risen Christ, most of whom, Paul said, were still alive at the time of his writing (1 Corinthians 15:6). Paul himself, once a persecutor of Christians, was converted after an encounter with the risen Christ.

THE PICTURE OF DEATH DEFEATED

Christianity proclaims that God's response to our fear of death is the death and resurrection of Christ. Through his death and resurrection Jesus conquered death. His resurrection leads us to say that evil, illness, sin, and death will never have the final word. There is always hope.

The Easter following Muhammad Ali's death, I was trying to give my congregation a picture or analogy of how Easter conveys the idea of a powerful victory over death itself. I reminded them of Ali's epic fight with Sonny Liston on May 25, 1965. It was a rematch, following Ali's surprise defeat of the former heavyweight champion the year before. Many people had dismissed Ali's first victory over Liston as a fluke. But in the first round of this rematch, the twenty-three-year-old Ali knocked Liston down for the count. Perhaps you've seen the iconic photograph of Ali standing over Liston shouting, "Get up and fight, sucker!" That's the image I have in my mind of Christ's defeat of death itself at Easter. His resurrection gives us hope that hatred, evil, illness, sin, and death will never have the final word. There is always hope, not only in this life but also in the next.

It was C. S. Lewis who once said that what we believe about death and the afterlife fundamentally changes how we live *this* life. If I believe that the Gospel writers and the apostles were telling the truth, and that Jesus died and rose again (as astounding as that may seem), and if I trust the words of Jesus himself about death and the afterlife, then I can face all of life, including every fear I describe in this book, with courage and hope.

Now, for some, a belief in the resurrection and eternal life leads to indifference about what happens on earth. I've heard some Christians speak as though they don't have to care about the suffering of others, for if those in extreme poverty die, they "get to go to heaven." I once heard a woman say that she didn't worry about the environment or any other temporal concerns because "this world is not my home." This is a gross misreading of the Gospels. It was Jesus who called us to care for the hungry, the thirsting, the naked, the sick, the immigrant, and the prisoner. And it was he who said that if we've been indifferent to the needs of our fellow human beings in this life, we'll have no part with him in the next one. Again, Jesus's focus was not on heaven—it was on how we live here on earth.

The promise of life beyond death shouldn't make us indifferent to the suffering of others; rather, it should lead us to great courage and risk taking in addressing the pain and anguish in this world.

"WHAT IS HEAVEN LIKE?"

I'm often asked what heaven is like. Actually, the Bible offers surprisingly little by way of description (because, as I've noted above, the primary concern of scriptures is not getting you to heaven). We see glimpses of heaven in Old Testament passages where the prophets speak of a coming age in which the earth has been completely restored to the idyllic state that God intended: "They shall beat their swords into plowshares, and their spears into pruning hooks: nation shall not lift up sword against nation, neither shall they learn war anymore" (Isaiah 2:4 and Micah 4:3). Isaiah 11:6 captures another glimpse of this peaceful age: "The wolf also shall dwell with the lamb, and the leopard shall lie down with the kid; and the calf and the young lion and the fatling together; and a little child shall lead them."

The prophet Isaiah paints an unforgettable picture of this

restored Eden, where, he declares, God will "prepare for all peoples a rich feast, a feast of choice wines, of select foods rich in flavor, of choice wines well refined. He will swallow up on this mountain the veil that is veiling all peoples, the shroud enshrouding all nations. He will swallow up death forever. The Lord God will wipe tears from every face; he will remove his people's disgrace from off the whole earth, for the Lord has spoken" (Isaiah 25:6–8). Heaven, or the age to come, is portrayed as a great feast, a party, with the finest wines and foods, where sorrow, grief, and death will be no more.

Jesus picks up this same theme in Matthew 22, describing heaven as a wedding reception. This analogy took on more meaning for me after our oldest daughter got married. LaVon and I, as the parents of the bride, put on the reception, inviting our family and closest friends, and our kids' closest friends. We had food and champagne and live music. We laughed and danced and hugged and celebrated. When LaVon and I finally collapsed into bed late that night, we looked at each other and agreed that this was one of the best nights of our lives. And that is the picture both Isaiah and Jesus use to describe the age to come—a party or banquet where you are surrounded by the people you love, celebrating with joy and laughter.

I have listened to dozens of stories of near-death experiences over the last thirty years of ministry. On several occasions people who were resuscitated told me of friends and family members who welcomed them as their life was slipping away, and of the beauty of the place they saw. What stood out to me, though, were the descriptions of laughter they heard, of singing and utter joy.

But what about pearly gates and streets of gold? Yes, Revelation uses this imagery, but, like all of the imagery used to describe the age to come, it is merely a way of saying, "Think of the most beautiful and treasured things you can in this life—the next life is even more beautiful than these!"

Perhaps the most important thing we can say about the afterlife is that God's will is done in that realm. We recognize this, and yearn for it to come true, when we pray as Jesus taught, "Thy kingdom come, *thy will be done, on earth as it is in heaven*" (emphasis added). Heaven is the place where God's will is always done—which is what makes it heaven.

One of my favorite stories, dating back a hundred years, tells of a man who was dying alone at home. His doctor, traveling by horse and buggy, came to make a house call. He went everywhere with his faithful dog, whom he left on the front porch as he entered the home of his patient. The patient, lying in bed, said to the doctor, "Doc, I'm scared. What's it going to be like on the other side?" At that moment the doctor's dog began scratching at the door and whining, hoping to be let in. The doctor said, "Do you hear my dog scratching at your door? He's never been in your house. He doesn't know anything about the inside of your home. Here's the only thing he knows: His master is on the other side of that door. And if his master is inside, it must be okay, and it is where he wants to be. That's what heaven is like."

Believing this about death changes how we face our mortality. It doesn't mean we have no fear, only that we're not controlled by fear. It means that, despite our fear, we can live with real hope. Our hope is not only for our own survival after death, but that we will see our loved ones again. Good-bye is not forever.

Perhaps no one cherishes the hope of heaven more than those who lose children. The pain of loss for the parents and grandparents is almost unbearable. Regrettably, common distortions of Jesus's message can add to the pain of the loss of a child. Some people will say, "It must have been the will of God" or "It was their time." I do not believe that God wills the death of children. I don't believe it was "their time." I don't believe God sends cars swerving into one another to take the life of his children—not as punishment, not to teach us a lesson, not to deepen our faith, and not because "he needs another angel in heaven." Just as you would never inject a terrible disease into a child, God would never place cancer cells into his children's bodies. For the very young, as for all of us, illness and accident are occasionally and tragically part of the human experience. The promise of heaven does not take away the terrible pain of saying good-bye to your child. But it does offer a ray of hope and an anchor that holds in the midst of the storm as we trust that our children or spouses or parents or friends were welcomed by Christ himself at their deaths and are in a place of unspeakable joy, seeing the things we only dream of on this side of eternity. I love how Paul, borrowing from Isaiah, expresses this hope that is so much greater than our capacity to grasp: "No eye has seen, nor ear heard, nor the human heart conceived, what God has prepared for those who love him" (1 Corinthians 2:9).

LIVING COURAGEOUSLY IN THE FACE OF DEATH

Kurt and Carrie Soper, a young couple in my congregation, have shown me what it looks like to feel fear yet to live courageously in the face of death. The Sopers were high school sweethearts and have been married for twelve years. They have a seven-year-old daughter, Ava. Five years ago, Kurt was on the fast track in his career when doctors diagnosed him with a rare form of cancer. He underwent thirteen surgeries, including a hemipelvectomy that removed his left leg all the way up to the hip. Several months ago, the doctors told Kurt and Carrie that there was nothing else they could do; his condition is terminal.

I've had the privilege of sitting with the Sopers in their home on several occasions, and now, more recently, at our local Hospice House. For much of his battle with cancer, Kurt focused on helping others. He volunteered at the hospital, seeking to bless and encourage others until the end of his journey. Neither Kurt nor Carrie believe God made Kurt sick, but they do draw comfort from trusting that God is with them, and sees them as his beloved children. The hope of the resurrection has not taken away the difficulty of their journey, but it does provide them comfort and courage in the midst of it. Kurt, Carrie, and Ava were all baptized recently.

Kurt noted as we spoke, "Cancer might have won this fight, but it didn't win the war. I know that I'm going to continue to live in heaven. That provides me with peace and comfort—though my life was cut short, that's not the end. I'll see my wife and daughter again." Carrie told me, "To me Easter is the most important time of year—even more so right now because of our journey. And that promise of Easter is the salvation in our pain."

For Christians, faith is more than a set of beliefs or expectations. It radically and convincingly changes how we face death—our own death and the death of those we love. With the psalmist we trust that "though I walk through the valley of the shadow of death, I will fear no evil; for Thou art with me."

Each Easter sermon I've preached for the last twenty-eight years—and most of the funeral services—end in the same way:

"People ask me from time to time, 'Adam, you seem intelligent. Do you *really* believe this stuff? That Jesus rose from the dead? That we live after death with God in heaven?' My answer is always the same. 'I not only believe it, I'm counting on it.'" And that faith leaves me unafraid in the face of death.

20

Living with Fear, Yet Unafraid

My life has been full of terrible misfortunes most of which never happened.

—MICHEL DE MONTAIGNE

The fear of the Lord is a fountain of life, turning people away from deathtraps.

—PROVERBS 14:27

OUR GRANDDAUGHTER, STELLA, SPENT THE NIGHT LAST weekend, as she does once or twice a month. She's three years old and as adorable as any three-year-old ever was. Each time we see her she is more talkative than the last. On this visit, she would come up to me and say, "Papa, I need a hug." Or she'd say, "I have a secret," and as I leaned forward she would whisper in my ear, "I love you." It doesn't get any better than that.

That night I told her bedtime stories, prayed with her, and kissed her good night. Then her Mimi came to do the same. Soon she was fast asleep. But at midnight she began to cry in her sleep. She was having a bad dream. I picked her up and held her tight. Rocking her in my arms, I told her "Papa is here; you don't have to be afraid. I've got you, safe in my arms." Only then, with her arms wrapped around my neck and my arms holding her tight, did she stop crying and fall back to sleep, knowing she was safe from whatever terrified her in her dreams.

We're not so different from little Stella. Throughout this book we've considered the variety of fears that keep us awake at night, robbing us of peace. Like Stella at midnight, we can be struck by terror about things we only imagine—false events appearing real. Or our fears can be grounded in something we've seen, heard, or felt. Some of these threats are real, and our fears trigger our body's fight-or-flight response seeking to deliver us from harm. But often our fear mirrors Michel de Montaigne's description of his life mentioned at the top of this chapter: "full of terrible misfortunes most of which never happened."

We've seen that our capacity to fear is a gift meant to help us, protect us, and motivate us. The challenge comes when we fear things that are not threats, or we exaggerate in our minds the magnitude of the threat or the odds that it will affect us. When we become fear-full, that which was intended to protect us ends up controlling us and robbing us of a full life.

Living unafraid, then, is not to live without fear; it is to live without being controlled and consumed by fear. It is to fear the right things and to allow appropriate fear to motivate us to action. The process of combating our fears will require work on our part. My aim in writing this book has been to help people understand some of the most common fears we wrestle with, to differentiate between things we should fear and false or exaggerated fears, and to find ways to cope with our fears that lead us to live with courage and hope.

Before I conclude, I'd like to consider one positive fear we're meant to cultivate and be shaped by—a fear that plays a key part in addressing and combating all our other fears. Scripture speaks of it as "fear of the Lord."

FEAR AS A FOUNTAIN OF LIFE

The idea of fearing God is perplexing to many today. Aren't we to love God? Doesn't one of the apostles actually define God himself as love? Why then would we fear God? I believe the confusion stems from common misunderstandings and, at times, misrepresentations.

Think of "Sinners in the Hands of an Angry God," the famous sermon delivered by the eighteenth-century Puritan Jonathan Edwards. Preaching at the First Church of Christ in Enfield, Connecticut, on July 8, 1741, Edwards sought to terrify his hearers into repentance with evocations of God's wrath. In one of the best-known parts of this sermon, he said, "The God that holds you over the Pit of Hell, much as one holds a Spider, or some loathsome Insect, over the Fire, abhors you, and is dreadfully provoked; his Wrath towards you burns like Fire; he looks upon you as worthy of nothing else, but to be cast into the Fire."

Perhaps the church folk at Enfield were much worse sinners than the tax collectors, drunkards, and prostitutes Jesus befriended, but Jesus never spoke to sinners with words like Edwards's. The only time Jesus took a tone anything remotely similar was when he challenged hypocritical religious leaders. To them, he repeatedly said, "Woe unto you, scribes, Pharisees, hypocrites!" (Matthew 23:13 ff.). Or, "I assure you that tax collectors and prostitutes are entering God's kingdom ahead of you" (Matthew 21:31b). Yet to ordinary folk, whatever their list of transgressions, Jesus routinely offered compassion, mercy, and grace.

In scripture, fear of the Lord is not primarily terror evoked by an angry God. It is reverence, respect, and awe inspired by a

God who is all-powerful and who not only created heaven and earth but continues to exercise dominion over them.

That's not to deny the just judgment and discipline of God. I'm reminded of this statement, found in both the Old and the New Testaments: "The Lord disciplines those he loves." LaVon and I disciplined our children when they were growing up. We did not want them to be terrified of us, but we did want them to take us seriously and to pay attention when we told them no. I did not often yell at my kids, but I remember one day when one of our daughters was five years old. She slipped from my grasp in a parking lot and ran out from between the cars just as another car was coming. I caught her, set her in front of me, and scolded her quite severely. "You could have been seriously hurt, even killed! Don't ever, ever, ever do that again. DO YOU UNDERSTAND ME?" My anger was driven by fear for what could have happened. I'd buried children who'd died after being hit by a car. I hoped to make her afraid enough—if not of the car, then of her dad's wrath—that she'd never do this again. That is certainly one sense of the fear of the Lord in scripture—a healthy fear of God's discipline, a discipline reflecting God's love and care for us.

Years later I had a similar conversation with that same daughter when she and a friend, both thirteen at the time, "borrowed" her friend's parents' car late one night and took it for a joyride. This time the punishment included being grounded for a period, and the threat of being grounded for the rest of her life, if she ever did this again. Once again, the discipline came not out of anger, but out of my love for her and my deep desire to keep her from harming herself or someone else.

SEIZED BY AWE AND REVERENCE

Yet there is another sense in which the Bible speaks of the fear of the Lord. The Hebrew word translated as "fear" is *yirah*. In the Bible, *yirah* certainly can mean the fear of punishment or discipline. But *yirah* also conveys being *awestruck*—seized by an appropriate reverence and respect.

Roman Catholics consider fear of the Lord to be one of the seven gifts of the Holy Spirit. Thomas Aquinas distinguished between "servile fear"—the fear of punishment—and "filial fear"—the respect a dearly loved child has for a parent. Filial fear is closely linked to another gift, the gift of piety, which is deep reverence for God. Filial fear, as noted above, is closely linked to wonder and awe.

I'm reminded of how, when some of the great men and women of the Bible had encounters with God, they hid their faces in fear or fell to their knees. Isaiah claimed he had a vision of God on his throne that left him shouting, "Woe is me! I am lost!" (Isaiah 6:5a). Being awestruck is the appropriate response to the beauty, majesty, wonder, glory, and power of God.

I sense the awesome power of God when I look at the universe that God has made. I live in the country, far from city lights. On moonless nights, the Milky Way runs like a glowing river across the sky—more than one hundred billion stars like our sun that make up our galaxy. And our galaxy is but one of at least one hundred billion galaxies. As I stand there looking up, I'm moved to think about the words of Isaiah: "Lift up your eyes and look to the heavens: Who created all these? He who brings out the starry host one by one and calls forth each of them by name. Because of his great power and mighty strength, not one of them is missing" (40:26). The spectacle of creation on those nights can lead me to cry out, with the psalmist, "O Lord, our Sovereign, how majestic is your name in all the earth!" (Psalm 8:9).

Last week I was leaving my office just as a terrible storm struck. It was accompanied by seventy-mile-per-hour winds, heavy rains, and the most beautiful lightning I've ever seen. I ran to my car, which was parked several hundred yards from the door of the church, as the lightning flashed and the thunder clapped all around me. I was terrified and in awe all at the same time. (I learned later that lightning had struck a light pole in our parking lot, frying the control board for our parking-lot lights.)

If we have eyes to see, these beautiful expressions of creation point to the awesome power of the God who made them. While we often emphasize the intimacy and love of God, we would do well to remember the awesome power and glory of God. And it should lead us to reverence, respect, awe, wonder, and worship, yet much of this is lost to Christians today. Some contemporary expressions of our faith seem to treat God more like a buddy, a boyfriend, or a girlfriend than as the God before whom the great men and women of faith have knelt and trembled, filled with awe.

But here's the surprising gift of just this kind of fear of the Lord: it may be the most important key to living unafraid with courage and hope.

Sister Irene Nowell writes that the "fear of the Lord is the awareness that God is God and I am not . . . I am glad that God is God and I am not!"* We sometimes act as though the world

---

* Irene Nowell, *Pleading, Cursing, Praising: Conversing with God through the Psalms* (Collegeville, MN: Liturgical Press, 2013), p. 53.

revolves around us, our experiences, and what we want. The fear of the Lord changes our perspective. The writer of Psalm 90 captures it well:

> *Before the mountains were brought forth,*
> *or ever you had formed the earth and the world,*
> *from everlasting to everlasting you are God.*
> *You turn us back to dust,*
> *and say, "Turn back, you mortals."*
> *For a thousand years in your sight*
> *are like yesterday when it is past,*
> *or like a watch in the night.*
>
> (PSALM 90:1–4)

Have you ever stood at the edge of the ocean and contemplated its depth and breadth, or looked up at the stars and pondered just how vast our universe is? Both remind me of just how small I am in the scheme of things and, at the same time, how great is the One who created both the heavens and the earth. The psalmist captures this feeling in Psalm 8:3–4,

> *When I look at your heavens, the work of your fingers,*
> *the moon and the stars that you have established;*
> *what are human beings that you are mindful of them,*
> *mortals that you care for them?*

Indeed, each of us is just one of seven billion people on earth, and our planet is only a speck in the cosmos. And yet, Psalm 8 continues, despite how small we are, and how vast God is, the God by whose power the universe is sustained actually does care about us. It is this sense of the fear of the Lord—the awareness of how great God is and how small I am—that calms my anxious heart and helps me to trust him when he says, "Be still, and know that I am God!"

FINDING GOD IN THE STORMS

I don't believe, despite what property insurance policies might say, that natural disasters are "acts of God." Though they can be terribly destructive to humans, most are increasingly predictable, naturally occurring phenomena that play some role in the equilibrium of our planet.

I wrote this chapter from Honduras. In 1998, Hurricane Mitch slammed into this Central American country. Torrential storms dropped over thirty-five inches of rain in a short period of time, causing massive mudslides, killing 7,000 people and leaving 1.5 *million* people homeless. The country was devastated. While some proclaimed that God brought this terrible disaster to punish, or to teach, or to accomplish some unforeseen purpose, meteorologists described it otherwise. They saw the hurricane as the predictable result of warm, moist air rising from the surface of the ocean. This phenomenon forms storm clouds that begin to rotate as a result of the earth's movement. Meteorologists do not see hurricanes as acts of God and neither do I.

Hurricane Mitch's impact was magnified in Honduras by the fact that millions had built makeshift homes along the side of volcanic mountains whose soil is prone to mudslides when oversaturated. While I don't believe God causes hurricanes, or that he intentionally guides them to strike certain nations, I do believe God is with those impacted by these storms, and that he is able to bring good from these natural disasters.

In 2005, I was a part of a team that drove to Bay St. Louis, Mississippi, to muck out homes flooded by Hurricane Katrina. One woman told me how she sat in the attic of her home as the water levels rose, desperately trying to get out and onto the roof, and not sure if she would live or die. She was terrified but kept praying, "I know, dear Lord, that my life is in your hands. If I live or I die, I belong to you, and even now, you are with me." As the water filled her home, she became convinced that she would die. Even then, she arrived at a sense of peace, believing God was with her in the darkness of her attic and that if she died she would be held in his strong arms and awaken in that place where death has been defeated and there is no more sorrow, suffering, or pain. But she survived, and several weeks later our team was there, scraping the mud from her home, tearing out the moldy Sheetrock, and helping her put her life back together.

Though storms may remind us of God's awesome power, God didn't cause Hurricane Katrina. But I do believe the Lord was present in the attic with that woman as the floodwater rose. I believe God was working by his Spirit to console her in what she believed were the final hours of her life. And I believe God showed up in the flesh, bearing shovels and offering aid through the teams of people who came to help afterward. For her, fear of the Lord was her awareness that God is greater than a hurricane, and that even if death should claim her, God is greater than death too.

In this she reminded me of Shadrach, Meshach, and Abednego, whom the Babylonian king Nebuchadnezzar threw into a fiery furnace because they refused to kneel before his golden idol. They feared God more than they feared the mighty Nebuchadnezzar. As they were given one last chance to kneel before the king, the three young Israelites proclaimed that they believed God would deliver them from the fiery furnace, but even if he did not they would not bow down to Nebuchadnezzar's gods or to his golden statue (Daniel 3).

Likewise, Daniel refused to turn away from God even when King Darius's officials conspired to have him thrown into a den of lions if he prayed to anyone other than their gods (Daniel 6). In the same way, Queen Esther refused to remain silent when an evil man plotted to kill the Jewish people (Esther 3–4). Though it could have cost her life, she spoke up to the king about what was happening, ultimately helping to save her people.

Did Shadrach, Meshach, Abednego, Daniel, and Esther know fear? Of course. But their fear of the Lord, and their trust in God's power and God's providence, gave them the courage to overcome their fears of fiery furnaces, lions, and angry kings.

NOT FEAR
/ love or
/ Trust /

The point is simple, but life-changing. When we fear God— when we revere, respect, and stand in awe of God—we fear everything else a little less. The more we trust in God, the less we fear what anyone or anything can do to us, the more we rest in God's peace, and the more we seek to do his will.

Perhaps this is why the writers of Proverbs noted the following: "The fear of the Lord is the beginning of wisdom" (Proverbs 9:10). "The fear of the Lord prolongs life" (Proverbs 10:27). "In the fear of the Lord one has strong confidence, and one's children will have a refuge. The fear of the Lord is a fountain of life" (Proverbs 14:26–27). And finally, this insight, which I especially love: "The fear of the Lord is life indeed; filled with it one rests secure" (Proverbs 19:23).

GOD'S WAYS OF WORKING IN OUR WORLD

That takes me back to how God works in the midst of the storms we face in life. In the aftermath of Hurricane Mitch, the Spanish Red Cross came to Honduras and built a village called Ciudad España, with new homes for ten thousand of those who lost everything to the storm. Out of the tragedy, a new community emerged. Two years later, members of our church came to Ciudad España to help build a church and the Juan Wesley school. This year, as I stood among the school's 377 students, I felt sincere gratitude and hope knowing that these children would be receiving an education that might have eluded them otherwise.

These children don't remember Hurricane Mitch—they were not alive at the time it struck. They don't know the hillside villages that were washed away. What they know is that they have a school with teachers who love them, a place where a solid education will provide an opportunity for a future with hope. God did not send Mitch to destroy their families' lives and homes. But out of the tragedy of Hurricane Mitch, God moved tens of thousands of people to get involved in positively impacting the affected communities in Honduras. Through these volunteers and public servants, and the hard work of the Honduran people, new homes, schools, medical clinics, and churches have been built, all of which give a new generation of children a chance at a brighter future.

Allow me to restate the point: God has the power to force even the most tragic of tragedies to serve his purposes. That's why, when we fear the Lord—when we share a holy reverence and awe of God, recognizing his power and his ability to bend even suffering, tragedy, and evil to accomplish his purposes—we can face life unafraid, even in the midst of storms.

THE ONE WHOSE PRESENCE IS ENOUGH

I love the story of the lake crossing in Matthew 8:23–27. Jesus is sleeping in the back of a boat as his disciples are rowing away. A fierce squall sweeps in. As the winds rise and waves threaten to swamp the boat, the disciples become increasingly afraid. Yet Jesus sleeps on. Finally, they rouse him, shouting, "Lord, save us!"

Here's what the text says happened next: "He said to them, 'Why are you afraid, you of little faith?' Then he got up and rebuked the winds and the sea; and there was a dead calm. They were amazed, saying, 'What sort of man is this, that even the winds and the sea obey him?' "

What just happened here? Jesus's friends were awestruck—first by their fear of the storm, then by their awe of the One who commanded the wind and the waves to be still.

I remember a woman in my congregation telling me that during her battle with cancer, when things seemed most frightening, she would think about this story in scripture, and she would pray, "Lord, I trust that you are in this boat with me. I belong to you. Please help me remember that you are here, and since you are here, somehow, this is going to be okay." Releasing our fears to God requires that we trust that God is always by our side, big enough to care for us, and stronger than any storm we might face.

Natural disasters aside, even when human beings misuse their freedom in ways that hurt others or that do not align with God's will, God is able to work through these acts to bring about his good purposes. Hence Paul famously wrote, "We know that God works all things together for good for the ones who love God, for those who are called according to his purpose" (Romans 8:28).

Do you see how awe, wonder, and trust in God's power lead us to *not* be afraid? Isaiah said it this way: "Surely God is my salvation; I will trust, and will not be afraid, for the Lord God is my strength and my might; he has become my salvation" (12:2). It is why the psalmist could write, "Even when I walk through the darkest valley, I fear no danger because you are with me" (Psalm 23:4). It is why the disciples, after Christ calmed the winds and the waves, would no longer be afraid as long Jesus was in the boat with them.

THE ABIDING TRUST THAT CHANGES EVERYTHING

I think about the Apostle Paul, who, while in a Roman prison awaiting news of the outcome of his trial—whether the Romans would execute him or set him free—wrote his famous "Epistle of Joy," the letter to the Philippians. In this letter, composed during the darkest of circumstances, Paul said again and again that the Philippians should "rejoice in the Lord." Concerning the possibility of his death, he noted that he would like to go on living so that he might continue to serve God, but he added that to him "to live is Christ and to die is gain" (Philippians 1:21). What faith he had in the awesome power of God to care for him, even if he died!

I've spoken throughout this book of the various fears that afflict us, shape us, shake us, and can so easily rob us of joy and keep us from experiencing the life God intends for us. I've uncovered a variety of insights, strategies, and practices that can help us to control our fears rather than let our fears control us. But I hope you don't miss what the biblical authors discovered: whenever fear, worry, or anxiety struck, their abiding trust in God's unfailing love and power changed everything.

And that takes me back to my granddaughter Stella's nightmare. When she felt herself held by her Papa, and heard me whispering in her ear, she was finally able to go back to sleep, knowing that she was safe in my arms, trusting that I was more powerful than the things she feared in her dreams. This is a glimpse of the kind of trust the biblical authors cultivated in

God, the kind of trust we might cultivate, that allows us to say with the prophet Isaiah, "Surely God is my salvation; I will trust, and will not be afraid."

This is what Paul was talking about when, from his prison cell in Rome, he wrote, "Don't be anxious about anything; rather, bring up all of your requests to God in your prayers and petitions, along with giving thanks. Then the peace of God that exceeds all understanding will keep your hearts and minds safe in Christ Jesus" (Philippians 4:6–7).

You and I will experience fear, but we don't have to be oppressed, defeated, or controlled by it. We can face our fears with faith, examine our assumptions in light of facts, attack our anxieties with action, and release our cares to God. And in doing this we will discover the "peace of God that exceeds all understanding." This peace allows us to live unafraid with courage and hope.

Acknowledgments

The idea for this book came from Roger Freet, my agent, at Foundry Literary. While fear has been the topic of many of my sermons over the years, it was Roger who proposed that I undertake a book-length exploration of how to live unafraid. Roger also connected me with Convergent Books and the Crown Publishing team at Penguin Random House. As a general-market Christian publisher, Convergent focuses on the wider audience I've devoted much of my life and ministry to reaching. Thank you, Roger, for your vision and persistence. This book would not have happened without you.

I'm grateful for Ginger Rothhaas, long-time parishioner and now a seminary student, who served as my research assistant, pulling together relevant books, articles, and other important resources. Right from the start, her own interest in the subject proved tremendously helpful in framing our project.

As executive editor at Convergent, David Kopp brought invaluable editorial skills and personal commitment to the undertaking, and throughout the process he helped me reach for the best book possible. Editor Derek Reed played a key role at the outset and brought his clear analysis through several rounds of revisions. With Dave, he helped to make this a stronger and more readable book. My sincere thanks to you both.

I'm grateful as well for the rest of the Convergent team. In particular, my thanks go to Tina Constable, publisher, for your leadership, vision, and personal passion for this book. My thanks also to Campbell Wharton, associate publisher; Megan Schumann, publicity director; Nick Stewart, marketing director; the cover design team of Chris Brand and Jessie Bright; and the entire Crown sales team in New York and Colorado Springs. I value and appreciate each of you, and your dedication to the success of *Unafraid* has been inspiring.

I'm grateful for Susan Salley and Abingdon Press for partnering with Convergent to prepare the leaders' guides and the videos that accompany this book for use in small groups, and for their work in developing the children and youth components that allow this resource to be a churchwide study in local congregations. Thank you, Susan!

This book draws upon twenty-eight years of ministry with the people of the United Methodist Church of the Resurrection. In so many ways this book has been shaped by my ministry with them and their willingness to share their lives with me.

Finally, I want to thank my family. My daughters, Danielle and Rebecca; my son-in-law, JT; my granddaughter, Stella; our dog, Maybelle; and most of all, my wife, LaVon, have taught me about life and love, about fear and courage. LaVon, to you I owe an immeasurable debt of gratitude for your ideas and support, for your sharing your personal story, and for giving up vacation time, days off, and evenings with me so that I could complete this endeavor. I love you so very much.

Appendix

31 DAYS OF SCRIPTURE READINGS ON FEAR

As I completed the manuscript for *Unafraid*, I began work on a daily devotional related to fear. Among the great spiritual resources that help combat fear are prayer and scripture reading. One way of reading the Bible that can be most impactful in helping us overcome fear is called *lectio divina*—I mentioned it briefly in chapter 5.

Below is a list of thirty-one scripture passages that offer reassurance in the face of fear—one selection for each day of the month. I invite you to read the day's scripture in the morning when you awaken, and to read the same passage again in the evening before sleep. Here, I'd like to walk you through a simple form of *lectio divina* that many people find helpful in allowing the scriptures to speak to them.

- Find a quiet place where you can be alone without interruption for at least fifteen minutes. Begin with prayer, something like "Lord, thank you for today. Thank you for . . . ," and then name five things you are thankful for—life itself, your family, nature, other good things. Even when you are worried or afraid, with a little effort you can think of five things for which you're genuinely grateful.

- Next, acknowledge to God that you are struggling with fear, worry, or anxiety. You don't need to spend a lot of time naming all of your fears—simply acknowledge that you are struggling. Then pray, "Lord, speak to me as I read these words of scripture. Help me to hear from you."
- Now read the scripture, noting any words or phrases that stand out to you. Underline them or write them down in a journal or on a notepad. You may get little from the scripture the first time through. After you've read it, pray again, "Lord speak to me as I read once more these words of scripture."
- Read the scripture again, this time aloud, slowly, listening as you read. Reading aloud can help focus our minds on what we're reading. Underline the words or phrases that stand out to you as you read the passage a second time.
- Now, one last time, pray, "Lord speak to me. I'm listening." Read the passage a third time, either silently or in a whisper. Again, underline or jot down those portions of the scripture that speak to you.
- Finally, pray once more, but this time use the words of the scripture text that you underlined or jotted down in your prayer, claiming for yourself the faith of the scripture writer and expressing your own faith in the One whom he wrote about. End with words like these, "Lord, I belong to you. Keep me safe in your arms. Help me to remember you are always by my side."

I encourage you not only to begin your day in this way, but to end the day this way too. When you're ready for bed, repeat the process, or the parts of it you find most helpful, before you turn out the light. Many people have told me that doing this before bed allows them to sleep better. It places in their subconscious words of hope and encouragement that help push back their fears as they sleep.

I encourage you to read from a modern translation of the Bible. The Common English Bible (CEB), the New Revised Standard Version (NRSV), or the New International Version (NIV) are all excellent translations.

DAY ONE: Deuteronomy 31:6. Moses is speaking to the Israelites just before his death. He is commissioning Joshua to lead the Israelites into battle in the Promised Land. Marching into war is frightening, but listen carefully to Moses's words to the Israelites.

DAY TWO: Joshua 1:9. God is reassuring Joshua as he is preparing to lead the Israelites into battle. God's promise to be with Joshua is the reason he can be "strong and courageous."

DAY THREE: Psalm 3. The Psalms were prayers written in the form of Hebrew poetry and often set to music. Their words capture the fears and faith not only of their authors but of all who have found comfort in them.

DAY FOUR: Psalm 56. Often the psalmists were facing enemies—other nations attacking Israel or others among their own people who were mistreating them. Several lines in this psalm, including verses 3 and 4, are powerful affirmations of trust in God.

DAY FIVE: Proverbs 3:25–26. The Proverbs represent the collected wisdom of ancient Israel. They reflect what the writers observed in their own lives and in the lives of others.

DAY SIX: Isaiah 12. Isaiah's words in this chapter promised a day when the people of Israel would be delivered from their enemies. The words were initially spoken in a time of great difficulty, and it was trusting in these words, in the midst of adversity, that gave peace in the face of the storm.

DAY SEVEN: Isaiah 41:8–10. To a people living in a very frightening and difficult time, Isaiah penned these words on behalf of God. As you read, imagine God speaking them to you.

DAY EIGHT: Matthew 8:23–27. As you read this story, bring to mind the storms in your own life. Christians believe Jesus is in the "boat" with them all the time.

DAY NINE: Matthew 10:26–33. Jesus tells us that even the hairs on our heads are numbered—an expression indicating that God knows us even better than we know ourselves.

DAY TEN: Matthew 14:22–33. In this scene at sea, Jesus comes to the disciples in the midst of the storm and bids Peter to walk on the water with him. You are Simon Peter in this story.

DAY ELEVEN: Matthew 28:1–10. Twice in this passage, which follows Jesus's resurrection after he had been crucified by the authorities, the women who had come to Jesus's tomb are told not to be afraid. How does the resurrection of Jesus deliver those who believe in it from fear?

DAY TWELVE: Luke 1:26–38. In this well-loved story, the young Mary is told by God's messenger that she will have a child. Both the appearance of the messenger and the nature of the message must have been frightening. We're often called to do things that are frightening. Mary simply trusted God.

DAY THIRTEEN: Luke 2:8–10. When the angels appeared to the shepherds to announce the birth of the Savior, the shepherds were terrified. How does this beloved story speak to us about fear and how we respond to it?

DAY FOURTEEN: Luke 5:1–11. After a miraculous catch of fish, Jesus calls four fishermen to be his disciples. Both the miracle and the calling likely made them afraid.

DAY FIFTEEN: Luke 12:4–7. You read Matthew's version of this already, but Luke's is slightly different. How does fear of the Lord actually decrease our other fears? See chapter 20 of *Unafraid*.

DAY SIXTEEN: Luke 12:22–34. Again, you're reading Luke's version of what you already read in Matthew, but it bears rereading.

DAY SEVENTEEN: John 6:16–21. You read this story in Matthew on day 10. Here's John's version of this important story. Imagine Jesus speaking these words to you.

DAY EIGHTEEN: John 14:27. Jesus spoke these words to his disciples just before his arrest and crucifixion to prepare them for what lay ahead. How do they speak to you?

DAY NINETEEN: Romans 8:14–17. How does being a child of God and having the Holy Spirit help us not to fear?

DAY TWENTY: Romans 8:28. This single verse is often quoted in unhelpful ways, but its underlying message is powerful. It is not teaching us that God wills everything that happens, but that God has a way of forcing good even from evil, tragedy, and pain.

DAY TWENTY-ONE: Romans 8:35–39. A powerful affirmation that we cannot be separated—cut off or somehow disqualified—from God's love by anything or anyone.

DAY TWENTY-TWO: Philippians 4:4–7. Read these beloved verses carefully. They include several important keys to living without fear.

DAY TWENTY-THREE: Philippians 4:8–9. Like yesterday's reading from Paul's letter to the Philippians, these verses contain a powerful key to finding peace.

DAY TWENTY-FOUR: Colossians 3:12–17. As you read, notice Paul's prescription for finding peace with others and with God in the face of fear.

DAY TWENTY-FIVE: 1 John 4:16–21 (with a special focus on verse 18). How do the love of God and the love of others drive out fear?

DAY TWENTY-SIX: Psalm 23. Notice the psalm opens with an affirmation about God, but when the psalmist turns to the subject of fear, he begins to speak directly to God. What do you take away from that?

DAY TWENTY-SEVEN: Psalm 55:1–5 and 16–19. Remember, the Psalms reflect the faith and life struggles of their authors, often in times of great adversity. Notice the psalmist prays evening, morning, and midday (the

Jewish day began at sunset). This threefold pattern of prayer is helpful in combating fear.

DAY TWENTY-EIGHT: Proverbs 29:25. This one short verse is worth meditating upon when you find yourself afraid of others.

DAY TWENTY-NINE: Isaiah 41:1–10. These are powerful words from God to the Israelites. Hear them as God's words to you.

DAY THIRTY: Isaiah 43:1–3a. These verses do not promise that you won't face adversity. Instead, God says that when (not if) you pass through waters and fires of trial, he will be with you and what you face will not destroy you.

DAY THIRTY-ONE: Revelation 21:3–4. These powerful verses paint a picture of a day when God will make all things new and there will be no more sorrow, suffering, or pain.

Now that you've completed these verses, I encourage you to read them again, looking for fresh insights and listening for God's voice and word in them. If you are not involved in a Bible study group, I encourage you to consider joining one. Reading the Bible with others is a powerful way to hear God speak through the Biblical text while making friends and meeting people who will stand with you, support you, and help you grow in your faith.

About the Author

REVEREND ADAM HAMILTON is senior pastor of the 20,000-member Church of the Resurrection outside Kansas City, the largest and most influential United Methodist congregation in the United States. He is a leading voice for reconciliation and church renewal in mainstream Christianity, and the author of twenty-five books, which together have sold more than two million copies. His recent releases prior to *Unafraid* include *Making Sense of the Bible* (HarperOne), *Creed: What Christians Believe and Why,* and *Moses: In the Footsteps of the Reluctant Prophet* (both from Abingdon Press).

The recipient of numerous awards and honorary degrees, Adam earned his master of divinity degree at Perkins School of Theology at Southern Methodist University, where he received the B'nai B'rith Award in Social Ethics. He graduated with honors from Oral Roberts University with a degree in pastoral ministry. Since 2010, he has spoken to more than 70,000 Christian leaders in 40 states on leadership and strategies for missional outreach.

Adam and his wife, LaVon, have two grown daughters and live in Leawood, Kansas.

Find him at AdamHamilton.org and cor.org, and on Facebook (Facebook.com/PastorAdamHamilton) and Twitter (@RevAdam Hamilton).